Graphic Quilts from Everyday Images

15 Patterns Inspired by Urban Life, Architecture, and Beyond

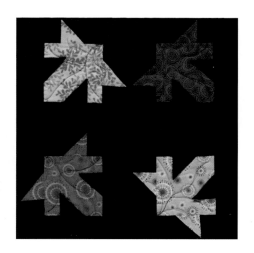

Heather Scrimsher

Martingale®
Create with Confidence

Dedication

To my husband, I owe you everything. Yin and yang.

To Tracy Gillies, I treasure all the awesome laughing sessions we had together.

Graphic Quilts from Everyday Images: 15 Patterns Inspired by Urban Life, Architecture, and Beyond
© 2014 by Heather Scrimsher

Martingale®
19021 120th Ave. NE, Ste. 102
Bothell, WA 98011-9511 USA
ShopMartingale.com

Printed in China

19 18 17 16 15 14   8 7 6 5 4 3 2 1

Library of Congress Cataloging-in-Publication Data is available upon request.

ISBN: 978-1-60468-430-8

Mission Statement

Dedicated to providing quality products and service to inspire creativity.

Credits

PUBLISHER AND CHIEF VISIONARY OFFICER: Jennifer Erbe Keltner

EDITOR IN CHIEF: Mary V. Green

DESIGN DIRECTOR: Paula Schlosser

MANAGING EDITOR: Karen Costello Soltys

ACQUISITIONS EDITOR: Karen M. Burns

TECHNICAL EDITOR: Ellen Pahl

COPY EDITOR: Marcy Heffernan

PRODUCTION MANAGER: Regina Girard

COVER AND INTERIOR DESIGNER: Connor Chin

PHOTOGRAPHER: Brent Kane

ILLUSTRATOR: Christine Erikson

Photos on pages 8, 13, 17, 22, 27, 32, 36, 40, 44, 50, 56, 60, 64, 67, and 70 by Heather Scrimsher

CONTENTS

INTRODUCTION

'll admit it up front; I'm a sucker for pretty things. From wine-bottle labels (who cares about the region or vintage—if the label is pretty, I might have to buy it), to artwork, to purses, to unique decor items, I'm always drawn to the stuff I find beautiful. I also have a strong desire to re-create cool things that I have experienced or seen. It's a short jump to translating things I've seen into my work with quilts.

This book is divided into sections. The first one, Enlarged Detail, focuses on enlarging a certain detail that I've photographed. Sometimes even the mundane can become extraordinary when enlarged or colored in a different way. These often turn out to be some of my favorite quilts.

The next section, Blocks and Repeats, uses blocks to play with a detail I take out of a photo. The detail can be manipulated and changed depending on what kind of block and placement is used. Working this way always reminds me of a kaleidoscope. I never quite know what I'm going to come up with when I begin.

The last section, Lines and Strips, focuses on the main elements of the photo or object. Sometimes there is too much detail to capture clearly, so some editing is necessary. Turning the lines of an object into strips instantly simplifies it and forces you to decide what is most important in an image.

Page through the book, look at the quilts, and check out the photos that inspired them. Sew the quilts as I did, or use entirely different fabrics to make them your own. Then peruse your travel photos, look at your favorite artwork, or consider your most cherished collectibles, and see how you can interpret them into a quilt.

TAKING INSPIRATION FROM PHOTOS

Nearly all my quilts start with a visual inspiration of some sort. Sometimes I find a photo that I love either because it's just pretty or because it evokes a certain feeling that I would love to immortalize in a quilt. For instance, I have a quilt hanging in my bedroom that was inspired by the sunset reflecting on glass. Every time I see it, I remember the inspiration photo and can feel the happy warmth of that sunset. Even if you don't take a lot of photographs, there are many ways to find excellent inspiration. On vacation, buy a book or postcard. Check out Pinterest. Cut photos out of magazines or catalogs. Any of these will work.

I ask myself several questions when I go about turning an inspiration into a quilt. I ask, "What is special about the photo?" Is it a color or perhaps a mood? Is it a memory? Or is it special just because it looks stunning? Sometimes I see a puzzle within the image, and that becomes the beginning of a quilt. How does everything fit together?

Once I answer those questions, I can decide if I want to capture the whole scene or focus on a small detail. Most of the time I find that a small detail is

enough. For instance, "Interlinked" (page 13) was based on a chain-link fence. I was daydreaming and kind of wondering who thought of twisting the metal in such a way that it all linked together. And how was it made? I went home and sketched a rough drawing of the linking metal. Then I started adding to the drawing, and the second link was created within the first. I moved from a sketch to graph paper and began to color in sections of my vision. Graph paper is a perfect intermediate medium because creating a quilt is easy once you've drawn the design onto grids. Then it's just a matter of doing the math—sometimes a lot of math.

So, if you want to re-create some of your favorite photos, start by identifying what appeals to you. Then roughly sketch out those parts. (There are no rules and no grading here. Trust me, my initial sketches are often a mess.) Next, apply your sketch to graph paper. Add some details or angled lines. Turn some pieces around. Then go fabric shopping and sew up your one-of-a-kind quilt!

Enlarged Detail

Quilts Based on a Photo Detail

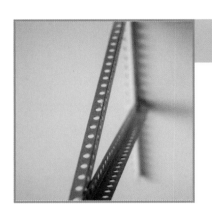

PUNCHED

INTERLINKED

POP BEADS

PROPELLER

STEEPLES

PUNCHED

This quilt is my interpretation of the brackets holding up a garage-door opener. Yes, it's slightly weird to notice such things, but I was sitting in my car one day and was fascinated by the shadows the brackets created as they crisscrossed each other. I snapped a photo and voilà, here is "Punched." I used Dale Fleming's 6-minute circle method, which makes it easy to piece rather than appliqué all the circles. It's a great technique—after the first couple, you'll be nodding along in appreciation.

Inspiration: garage-door brackets

Materials

Yardage is based on 42"-wide fabric.

2⅞ yards of light-aqua solid for background

2⅝ yards of gray solid for blocks and binding

⅝ yard of teal print for circles

⅝ yard of aqua print for circles

3⅞ yards of fabric for backing

68" x 76" piece of batting

Freezer paper

Template plastic

Paper scissors

Starch (optional)

Glue stick

Zipper foot

Cutting

From the gray solid, cut:
41 squares, 7½" x 7½"
7 strips, 2½" x 42"

From the teal print, cut:
21 squares, 5½" x 5½"

From the aqua print, cut:
20 squares, 5½" x 5½"

From the light-aqua solid, cut:
12 strips, 6½" x 42"; crosscut into:
    7 strips, 6½" x 30½"
    1 strip, 6½" x 24½"
    6 rectangles, 6½" x 18½"
    3 rectangles, 6½" x 12½"
    4 squares, 6½" x 6½"
4 squares, 9¾" x 9¾"; cut in quarters diagonally to yield 16 side setting triangles
2 squares, 5¼ x 5¼"; cut in half diagonally to yield 4 corner triangles

"Punched," designed, pieced, and quilted by Heather Scrimsher

Finished quilt: 60" x 68½"

Making the Circle Blocks

1 Trace the pattern on page 12 onto template plastic and cut out to make a 4" circle template.

2 Using paper scissors, cut two 6½" squares of freezer paper. Layer them, placing the shiny side next to a dull side, and use your iron to fuse them together. Place the circle template on the dull side of the freezer-paper squares and trace. Carefully cut out the center circle with paper scissors, maintaining a clean line. Keep the center circle handy.

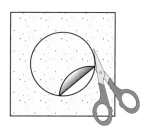

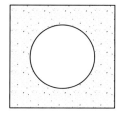

3 Lay a gray 7½" square on your ironing surface (wrong side up, if using a print). Center the freezer-paper template on top, with shiny side down. Press to adhere the template to the wrong side of the fabric. Using sharp scissors, make a snip in the center of the fabric, and then cut away a circle shape, leaving at least ⅝" of fabric around the inner edge of the template. Make clips around the curved edge, stopping ⅛" from the template edge.

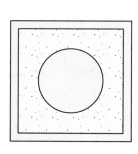 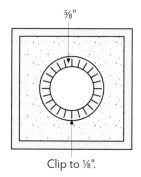

⅝"

Clip to ⅛".

4 With the template and fabric right side down on your ironing surface, fold the clipped curved edge over the edge of the freezer-paper template and press in place. Spray lightly with starch, if desired, and then press again to secure.

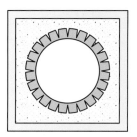

5 Center the freezer-paper circle from step 2 on the right side of a teal 5½" square. Run a light line of glue stick around the fabric just outside the circle. Place the gray unit from step 4 with freezer paper still attached onto the teal square with both fabrics facing right side up, using the freezer-paper circle as a placement guide. Press with your fingertips to adhere the layers together. Remove the freezer-paper circle. Then carefully lift the gray fabric up and gently remove the freezer paper, leaving a porthole with the teal print showing through. Press with a dry iron to set the glue.

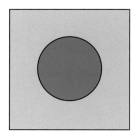

6 Install the zipper foot on your sewing machine to prepare for stitching the circles. With the right side of the unit from step 5 facing up, lift the gray-solid piece to reveal the crease line around the circle. Position the needle in the crease, adjusting the needle position if necessary. Sew around the circle, stitching slowly and moving the gray fabric out of the way as you go. When the stitching is complete, remove the unit from the machine and trim the seam allowance on the wrong side to ¼".

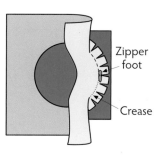

Zipper foot

Crease

7 Press the block and trim it to 6½" square, keeping the circle centered.

8 Repeat steps 2–7 using the remaining gray, teal-print. and aqua-print squares. You can reuse the freezer-paper template three or four times before making a new one. Make a total of 41 circle blocks.

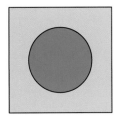
Make 21.

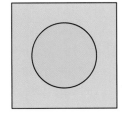
Make 20.

Assembling the Rows

This quilt is assembled in diagonal rows. Some of the circle blocks along the edges will be trimmed after sewing the rows together. Press seam allowances after each step, following the arrows in the diagrams.

1 Join a light-aqua 6½" square and two light-aqua side setting triangles as shown, right sides together. Make two.

Make 2.

2 Sew a light-aqua side setting triangle to one end of a light-aqua 6½" x 18½" rectangle and sew a teal block to the opposite end as shown. Sew this to one of the units from step 1, matching centers.

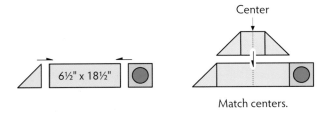
Match centers.

3 Sew two light-aqua side setting triangles, the light-aqua 6½" x 24½" strip, and a teal block together as shown.

4 Sew two teal blocks and a light-aqua 6½" x 30½" strip, 6½" square, and side setting triangle together as shown.

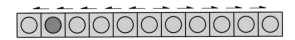

5 Sew 10 aqua blocks and one teal block together as shown.

6 Sew three teal blocks and a light-aqua side setting triangle, 6½" square, 6½" x 30½" strip, and 6½" x 18½" rectangle together as shown.

7 Sew three teal blocks and a light-aqua side setting triangle, 6½" x 12½" rectangle, 6½" x 30½" strip, and 6½" x 18½" rectangle together as shown.

6½" x 12½"

8 Sew three teal blocks, two light-aqua 6½" x 18½" rectangles, and a light-aqua 6½" x 30½" strip together as shown.

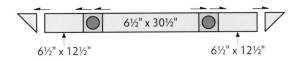

9 Sew two teal blocks, two light-aqua side setting triangles, two light-aqua 6½" x 12½" rectangles, and a light-aqua 6½" x 30½" strip together as shown.

10 Sew 10 aqua blocks and one teal block together as shown.

11 Sew two teal blocks, two light-aqua side setting triangles, and a light-aqua 6½" x 30½" strip together as shown.

12 Sew two teal blocks and a light-aqua 6½" x 30½" strip together as shown.

13 Sew two light-aqua side setting triangles and a light-aqua 6½" x 18½" rectangle together as shown.

Assembling the Quilt

1 Arrange the rows and light-aqua corner triangles as shown in the assembly diagram. Sew the rows together. Press the seam allowances in one direction.

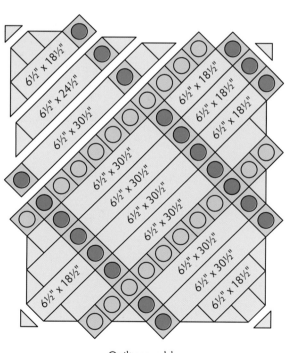

Quilt assembly

2 Press the quilt top well. Using a rotary cutter and ruler, trim the blocks along the edges of the quilt, making sure to leave a ¼" seam allowance beyond the corners of the rows.

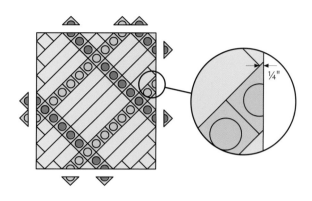

3 Referring to "Finishing Your Quilt" on page 78, quilt as desired and bind using the gray 2½"-wide strips.

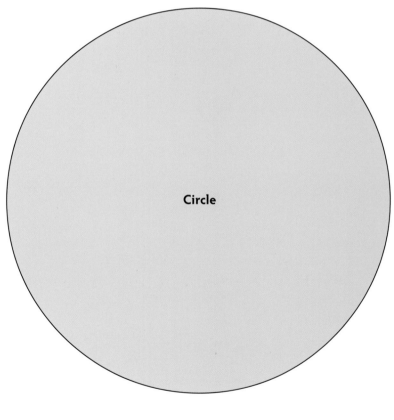

Circle

INTERLINKED

Chain-link fences are cold and slightly on the ugly side—in my opinion. But it's interesting to try tracing the path of the wire as it travels throughout the links. How it folds on itself and around the piece of metal next to it is amazing. In my quilt, I focused on the design and interaction of a single link. The result is striking and dramatic, inspired by something quite the opposite.

Inspiration: chain-link fence

Materials

Yardage is based on 42"-wide fabric.

2½ yards of gray print for background

1¼ yards of pink solid for wide link

⅝ yard of purple solid for narrow link

⅝ yard of fabric for binding

3¼ yards of fabric for backing

58" x 69" piece of batting

Cutting

From the gray print, cut:

7 strips, 2⅞" x 42"; crosscut into 86 squares, 2⅞" x 2⅞"

6 strips, 2½" x 42"; crosscut into:
 30 rectangles, 2½" x 4½"
 28 squares, 2½" x 2½"

4 strips, 6½" x 42"; crosscut into:
 8 rectangles, 6½" x 13½"
 2 rectangles, 6½" x 8½"
 4 rectangles, 6½" x 7½"

1 strip, 3½" x 42"; crosscut into 4 rectangles, 3½" x 6½"

1 strip, 5½" x 42"; crosscut into:
 1 rectangle, 5½" x 12½"
 2 rectangles, 5½" x 7½"
 2 rectangles, 2½" x 5½"

1 strip, 4½" x 42"; crosscut into 4 rectangles, 4½" x 7½"

3 squares, 4" x 4"

Continued on page 15

"Interlinked," designed, pieced, and quilted by Heather Scrimsher

Finished quilt: 50½" x 61½"

Continued from page 13

From the pink solid, cut:

- 4 strips, 2⅞" x 42"; crosscut into 48 squares, 2⅞" x 2⅞"
- 8 strips, 2½" x 42"; crosscut into 44 rectangles, 2½" x 6½"
- 2 rectangles, 6½" x 8½"
- 2 rectangles, 5½" x 8½"
- 4 squares, 2½" x 2½"

From the purple solid, cut:

- 4 strips, 2⅞" x 42"; crosscut into 44 squares, 2⅞" x 2⅞"
- 3 squares, 4" x 4"
- 2 rectangles, 2½" x 5½"

From the binding fabric, cut:

- 6 strips, 2½" x 42"

Making the Units

1 Referring to "Half-Square-Triangle Units" on page 77, layer a pink and a gray 2⅞" square together to make two half-square-triangle units. Repeat to make 88. Label these A. Repeat with 42 purple and 42 gray 2⅞" squares to make 84 half-square-triangle units. Label these B.

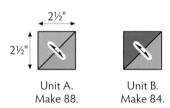

Unit A.
Make 88.

Unit B.
Make 84.

2 Layer a purple and a gray 4" square to make two half-square-triangle units. Repeat to make four. Trim to 2⅞" square. Layer these pieced squares with pink 2⅞" squares; draw a diagonal line on the wrong side of each pink square so that it is perpendicular to the seam of the half-square triangle. Sew and cut as before to make eight units as shown. Label these C.

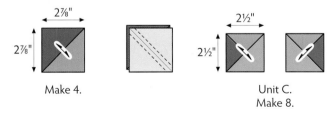

Make 4.

Unit C.
Make 8.

3 Repeat step 2 with one purple and one gray 4" square, and two purple 2⅞" squares. Make four units as shown and label these D.

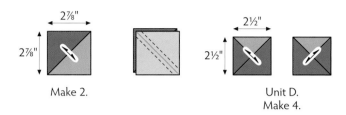

Make 2.

Unit D.
Make 4.

Assembling the Quilt

You will assemble the quilt in rows. Press seam allowances in opposite directions within each row and from row to row, except row 6, where you'll press seam allowances open.

1 **Row 1.** Sew together two gray 3½" x 6½" rectangles, four gray 2½" x 4½" rectangles, four gray 2½" squares, one gray 6½" x 8½" rectangle, six pink 2½" x 6½" rectangles, 12 A units, and 12 B units as shown. Make two rows.

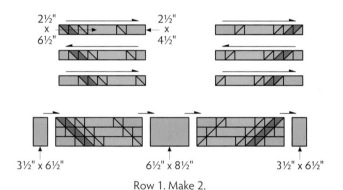

3½" x 6½"   6½" x 8½"   3½" x 6½"

Row 1. Make 2.

2 **Row 2.** Sew together two gray 4½" x 7½" rectangles, three gray 2½" x 4½" rectangles, two gray 2½" squares, four pink 2½" x 6½" rectangles, eight A units, and eight B units as shown. Make two rows.

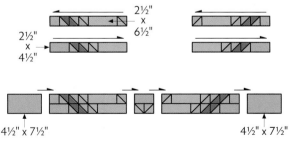

4½" x 7½"   4½" x 7½"

Row 2. Make 2.

3 **Row 3.** Sew together two gray 6½" x 13½" rectangle, two gray 2½" x 4½" rectangles, two gray 2½" squares, two pink 2½" squares, one pink 6½" x 8½" rectangle, four A units, 10 B units, and two C units as shown. Make two rows.

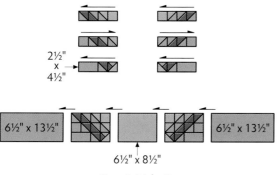

Row 3. Make 2.

4 **Row 4.** Sew together two gray 6½" x 13½" rectangles, two gray 2½" x 4½" rectangles, two gray 2½" squares, six pink 2½" x 6½" rectangles, eight A units, two C units, and two D units as shown. Make two rows.

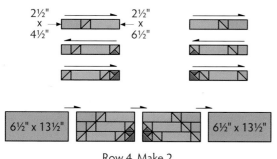

Row 4. Make 2.

5 **Row 5.** Sew together two gray 6½" x 7½" rectangles, four gray 2½" x 4½" rectangles, four gray 2½" squares, six pink 2½" x 6½" rectangles, 12 A units, and 12 B units as shown. Make two rows.

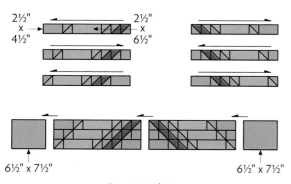

Row 5. Make 2.

6 **Row 6.** Sew together two gray 5½" x 7½" rectangle, two gray 2½" x 5½" rectangles, one gray 5½" x 12½" rectangle, two pink 5½" x 8½" rectangles, and two purple 2½" x 5½" rectangles as shown. Make one row. Press the seam allowances open.

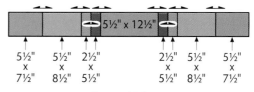

Row 6. Make 1.

7 Arrange the rows as shown in the assembly diagram. Sew the rows together. Press seam allowances in one direction.

8 Refer to "Finishing Your Quilt" on page 78. Quilt as desired and bind using the 2½"-wide strips.

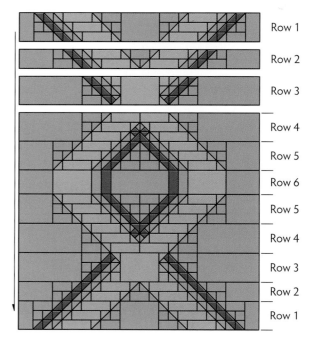

Quilt assembly

POP BEADS

I have a string of beads hanging in my sewing studio that remind me of Mardi Gras and the party that seems to define all of New Orleans. I love them because they're my favorite color, teal, and they remind me of little hexagons. I've tried English paper piecing to create hexagons, but had a hard time getting into it. (Maybe that's because I'm of Irish descent!) This quilt has hexagons, but involves no paper, English or otherwise.

Inspiration: Mardi Gras–style beads

Materials

Yardage is based on 42"-wide fabric.

3 yards of dark-plum solid for background

⅔ yard of medium-green solid for bead blocks

⅜ yard of dark-green solid for bead blocks

¼ yard of fuchsia solid for sashing

⅝ yard of fabric for binding

3⅓ yards of fabric for backing

60" x 70" piece of batting

Template plastic *OR* Jaybird Quilts Hex N More ruler

Cutting

Make templates by tracing the A and B triangle patterns on page 21 onto template plastic and cutting them out. If you have the Hex N More ruler, use the 3½" triangle lines for cutting A pieces and make a B template only for the setting triangles.

From the medium-green solid, cut:
   6 strips, 3½" x 42"; cut into 84 A triangles

From the dark-plum solid, cut:
   2 strips, 4½" x 42"
   2 rectangles, 27½" x 42"
   4 strips, 3½" x 42"; cut into 80 B triangles
   2 strips, 2½" x 42"
   4 strips, 1½" x 42"
   2 rectangles, 5" x 6½"
   2 squares, 2½" x 2½"

Continued on page 19

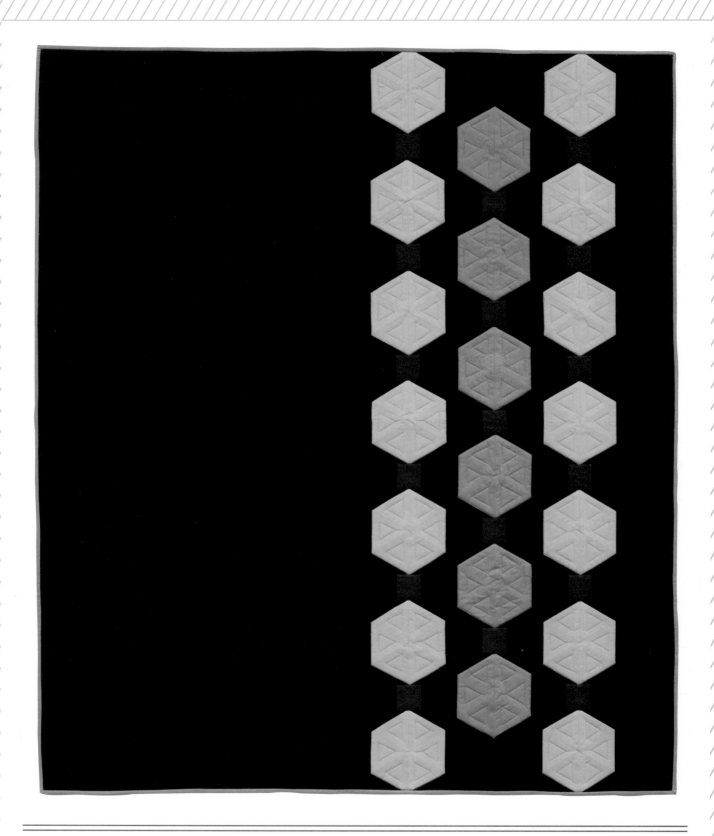

"Pop Beads," designed and pieced by Heather Scrimsher, machine quilted by Pat Derry

Finished quilt: 51½" x 61"   **Finished block:** 6" x 7"

Continued from page 17

From the dark-green solid, cut:
　3 strips, 3½" x 42"; cut into 36 A triangles

From the fuchsia solid, cut:
　1 strip, 2½" x 42"
　1 square, 2½" x 2½"

From the binding fabric, cut:
　6 strips, 2½" x 42"

Making the Bead Blocks

1 Place two medium-green A triangles right sides together, aligning the raw edges. Stitch from the flat top down one side as shown. Repeat to make a second pair. Press the seam allowances open.

 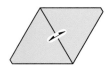

Make 2.

2 Sew a third medium-green A triangle to each pair from step 1, aligning raw edges along the base of the triangles. Press the seam allowances open.

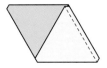 

Make 2.

3 Sew the two units together, matching centers, to make a hexagon. Press the seam allowances open.

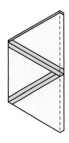 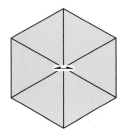

4 To create a rectangular block, sew a dark-plum B triangle to each of four sides as shown. Press the seam allowances toward the hexagon after adding each triangle. The top and bottom of the hexagon will have several seam allowances overlapping after the setting triangles are added—this is normal.

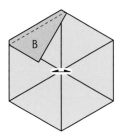 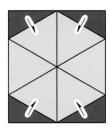

5 Repeat steps 1–4 to make a total of 14 medium-green blocks and six dark-green blocks.

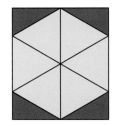 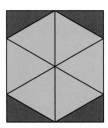

Make 14.　　　　Make 6.

Assembling the Quilt

1 Sew a dark-plum 2½" x 42" strip to each long side of the fuchsia 2½" x 42" strip to make a strip set. Press the seam allowances toward the dark-plum strips. Cut 16 segments, 2½" wide. If you can cut an extra segment, do so. If not, sew a dark-plum 2½" square to each side of the fuchsia 2½" square to make the final segment, for a total of 17.

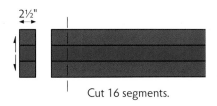

2½"

Cut 16 segments.　　　　Make 1.

2 Join seven medium-green hexagon blocks and six segments from step 1 as shown. Note that the tips of the hexagons should be pointing up and down. Press the seam allowances toward the segments. Make two vertical rows.

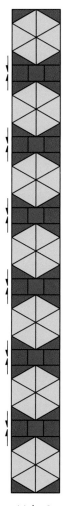

Make 2.

3 Join six dark-green hexagon blocks and five segments from step 1 to make a vertical row. Sew a dark-plum 5" x 6½" rectangle to each end of the row. Press the seam allowances toward the segments and rectangles.

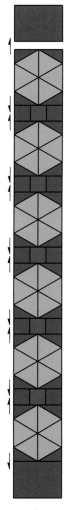

Make 1.

Design Options

Don't be afraid to take an element of a quilt and use it in another project. Your favorite part of a quilt pattern can be turned into something that takes an afternoon and features one of your favorite fabrics, like a pretty pillow decorating a comfy chair. "Pop Beads" can be easily altered into a table runner, pillow, or even the front of a bag. Simply take portions of the pattern and add background to create your desired shape. I made a holiday table runner that features a single line of hexagons similar to the ones featured in "Pop Beads."

4 Join two dark-plum 1½" x 42" strips end to end, and then trim to 1½" x 61". Make two.

5 Join the hexagon rows and the plum strips with the dark-green hexagon row in the middle. Press the seam allowances toward the plum strips.

6 Join the two dark-plum 4½" x 42" strips end to end, and then trim to 4½" x 61". Sew this strip to the right side of the hexagon rows. Press.

7 Join the two dark-plum 27½" x 42" rectangles and trim to 27½" x 61", centering the seam if desired. Sew this piece to the left side of the quilt. Press.

8 Refer to "Finishing Your Quilt" on page 78. Quilt as desired and bind using the 2½"-wide strips.

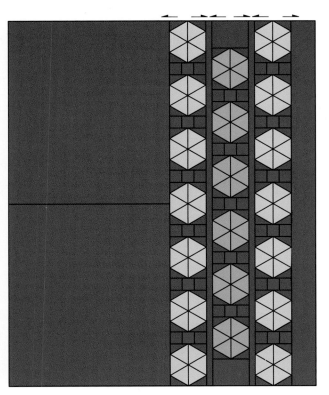

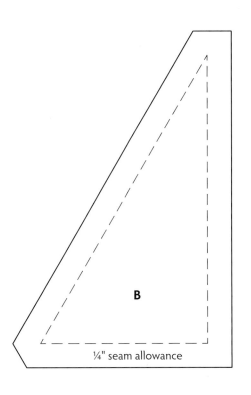

B

¼" seam allowance

Quilt assembly

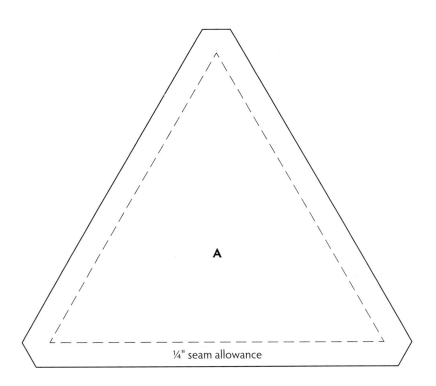

A

¼" seam allowance

PROPELLER

A irplanes and fans both have spinning blades, and as a child I loved watching propellers and fan blades go round and round; I was mesmerized by the way they appear to almost stand still when spinning at just the right speed. This quilt, inspired by those objects, is the perfect size for a baby, with room to grow.

Inspiration: Lego plane

Materials

Yardage is based on 42"-wide fabric. Fat quarters measure 18" x 21" and fat eighths measure 9" x 21".

2⅝ yards of gray solid for background

1 fat quarter *each* of 2 yellow prints for propeller blades

1 fat quarter *each* of 2 orange prints for propeller blades

1 fat eighth *each* of 2 yellow prints for streamers

1 fat eighth *each* of 2 orange prints for streamers

⅝ yard of fabric for binding

3⅓ yards of fabric for backing

60" x 60" piece of batting

Template plastic

Cutting

Make templates A and B from template plastic using the patterns on pages 25 and 26.

From the gray solid, cut:
 4 strips, 9½" x 26"
 4 strips, 6½" x 26"
 4 squares, 9" x 9"
 8 using template A

From *each* of the orange and yellow fat quarters, cut:
 2 using template B (8 total)

From *each* of the orange and yellow fat eighths, cut:
 2 strips, 2½" x 21" (8 total)

From the binding fabric, cut:
 6 strips, 2½" x 42"

"Propeller," designed, pieced, and quilted by Heather Scrimsher

Finished quilt: 51½" x 51½"

Assembling the Quilt

1 Referring to "Drunkard's Path Units" on page 77, join a print B piece to a gray A piece along the curved edges. Press the seam allowances toward the A piece. Make two of each print for a total of eight Drunkard's Path units. Press the seam allowances toward the gray solid in one of each print and toward the print in the other.

Make 2 of each print.

2 Trim and square each unit to 9" x 9". Trim the print corner first; the print should measure 8¼" along the side. A square ruler, at least 9½" x 9½", is very helpful for this. Trim along the right side and then the top of the unit. Then rotate the block 180° and align the trimmed corner with the 9" marks on the ruler to finish trimming the unit to 9" square.

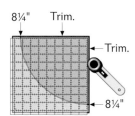 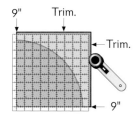

3 Join two matching units along the print sides to create a half circle. Pay special attention to where the print B pieces meet. The seams should butt together, helping you match the seam allowances perfectly to create a smooth curve. Press the resulting seam allowances open. Make four half-circle units.

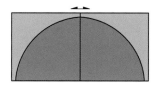

Make 4.

4 Sew a gray 9" square to the left side of each half-circle unit and press the seam allowances toward the square. Make four.

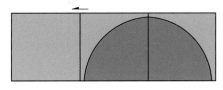

Make 4.

5 Sew two matching-print 2½" x 21" strips together end to end to make one long strip. Make four. Press and trim the strips to 2½" x 26".

6 Sew a gray 9½" x 26" strip and a gray 6½" x 26" strip to opposite sides of each strip from step 5. Press the seam allowances toward the print strip. Make four.

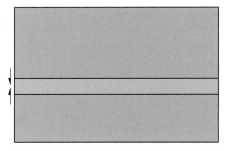

Make 4.

7 Sew a strip unit from step 6 to the top of a half-circle unit of the opposite color, ensuring the gray 6½"-wide strip is next to the top of the half circle. Press toward the strip unit. Make four.

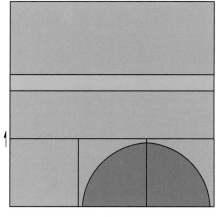

Make 4.

8 Arrange the units from step 7 together as shown. Join the units in pairs and then sew the two halves together. Press the seam allowances open.

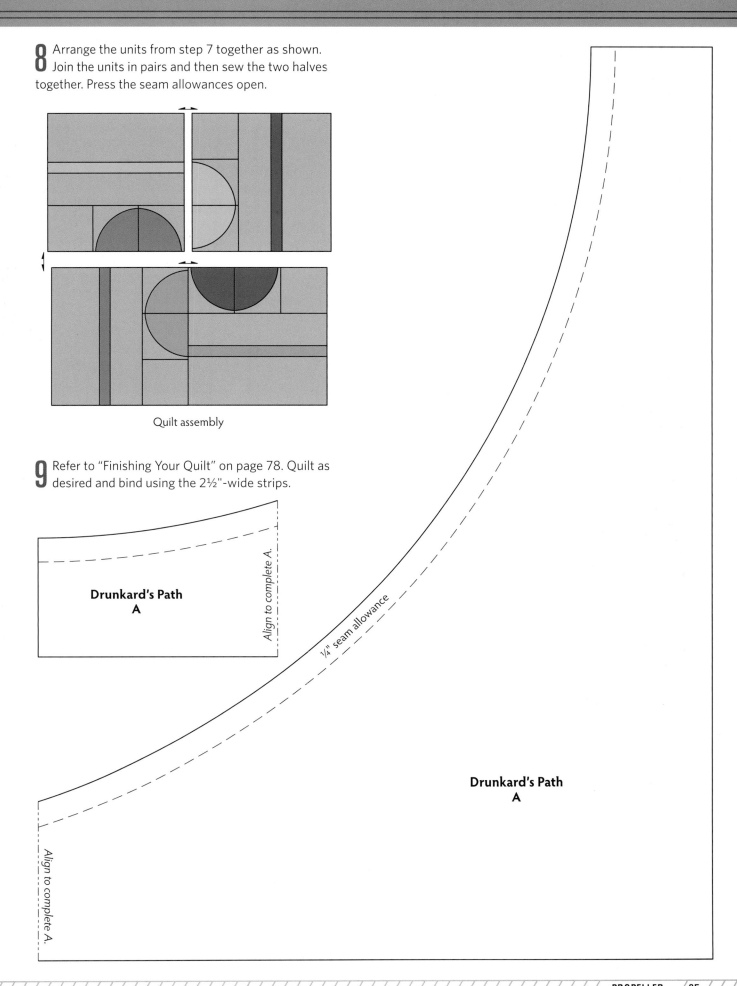

Quilt assembly

9 Refer to "Finishing Your Quilt" on page 78. Quilt as desired and bind using the 2½"-wide strips.

Drunkard's Path
A

Align to complete A.

¼" seam allowance

Drunkard's Path
A

Align to complete A.

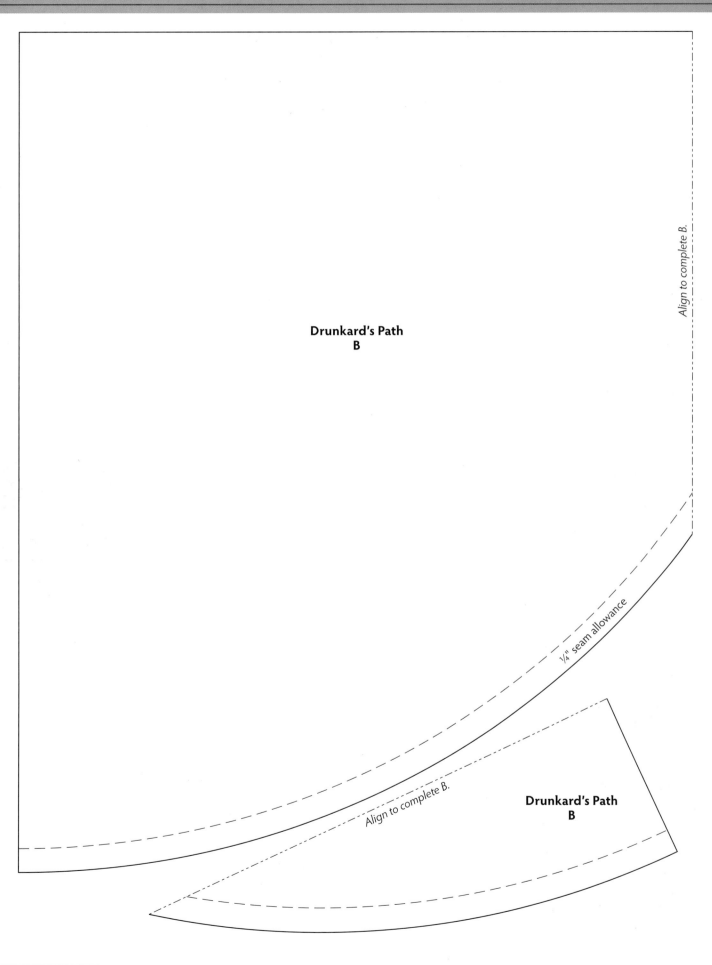

Drunkard's Path
B

Align to complete B.

¼" seam allowance

Align to complete B.

Drunkard's Path
B

STEEPLES

've lived in several different places in the United States, and each area has certain architecture and landscape features that create a unique regional feel. The South, where I currently live, is no different. I am enchanted by the country roads here. Around any bend, you can encounter a pristine little white church, set in a green field, always with a charming steeple. Half-square-triangle units in a variety of neutral shades create the rooflines and tops of the steeples in my quilt interpretation.

Inspiration: country church

Materials

Yardage is based on 42"-wide fabric.

3⅞ yards of green solid for background and binding

⅜ yard *each* of 4 light solids for steeples and rooftops

3½ yards of fabric for backing

62" x 70" piece of batting

Cutting

From *each* of the 4 light solids, cut:

1 strip, 4⅞" x 42"; crosscut into 8 squares, 4⅞" x 4⅞" (32 total; 2 are extra)

1 strip, 4½" x 42"; crosscut into 4 squares, 4½" x 4½" (16 total; 2 are extra)

From the scraps of the light solids, cut a *total of*:

4 rectangles, 2½" x 4½"

4 squares, 2½" x 2½"

2 squares, 2⅞" x 2⅞"

From the green solid, cut:

4 strips, 4⅞" x 42"; crosscut into 26 squares, 4⅞" x 4⅞"

2 strips, 4½" x 42"; crosscut into 16 squares, 4½" x 4½"

2 rectangles, 14½" x 24½"

2 rectangles, 8½" x 20½"

4 rectangles, 8½" x 14½"

4 squares, 8½" x 8½"

1 strip, 4½" x 42"; crosscut into 4 rectangles, 4½" x 8½"

2 strips, 4½" x 28½"

2 strips, 2½" x 24½"

4 squares, 2½" x 2½"

2 squares, 2⅞" x 2⅞"

2 rectangles, 2½" x 4½"

7 strips, 2½" x 42"

"Steeples," designed, pieced, and quilted by Heather Scrimsher

Finished quilt: 56½" x 64½"

Making the Units

1 Layer a light 4⅞" square right sides together with a green 4⅞" square. Referring to "Half-Square-Triangle Units" on page 77, make two half-square-triangle units. Repeat to make 52. You will have two extra, but that allows you to pick and choose a bit when combining the lights. Repeat with four light 4⅞" squares to make four half-square-triangle units with a light solid on each side.

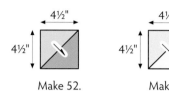

Make 52.   Make 4.

2 Sew a light 2½" square to a green 2½" square. Press the seam allowances toward the light square. Add a light 2½" x 4½" rectangle to the bottom. Press the seam allowances toward the rectangle. Make two of these units. Repeat to make two units with the green on the opposite side, and press the final seam allowances toward the squares.

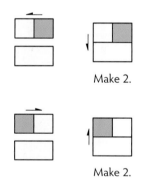

Make 2.

Make 2.

3 Make four half-square-triangle units with two light and two green 2⅞" squares. Press the seam allowances toward the green fabric. Join two half-square-triangle units as shown. Press the seam allowances open. Sew a green 2½" x 4½" rectangle to the top of the unit to make a peak. Press the seam allowances toward the green rectangle. Make two peaks.

Make 2.

Assembling the Quilt

This quilt is assembled in sections. You'll make one half and repeat to make the second half. One half is then rotated and the two halves are sewn together with a horizontal seam.

1 Make the steeple section by joining five light 4½" squares in random order. Add a peak unit as shown to make a steeple. Press the seam allowances in one direction.

2 Sew a green 2½" x 24½" strip to the right edge and a green 14½" x 24½" rectangle to the left edge of the steeple. Press the seam allowances toward the green fabric. Sew a green 8½" x 20½" rectangle to the top of the section. Press.

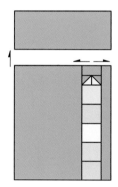

3 Sew two light 4½" squares together and add green 8½" x 14½" rectangles to each side. Press.

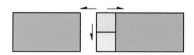

4 Sew two light half-square-triangle units together with two units from step 2 of "Making the Units" at left. Press the seam allowances as shown. Add two green 4½" squares to each side, and then add a green 8½" square to each side.

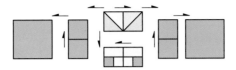

5 Arrange 24 light/green half-square-triangle units, four green 4½" squares, and two green 4½" x 8½" rectangles in four rows as shown. Sew the units into rows; press the seam allowances in opposite directions from row to row. Sew the rows together and press the seam allowances in one direction.

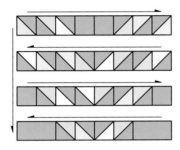

6 Sew the units from steps 3, 4, and 5 together as shown. Press.

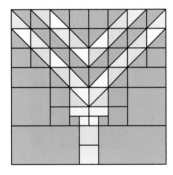

7 Sew a light/green half-square-triangle unit to the end of a green 4½" x 28½" strip. Press.

8 Sew the unit from step 7 to the left side of the section from step 6. Press and join to the steeple unit from step 2 to make half of the quilt.

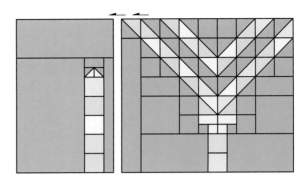

9 Repeat steps 1–8 to make the second half of the quilt. Rotate one half and sew the halves together. Press the seam allowances to one side.

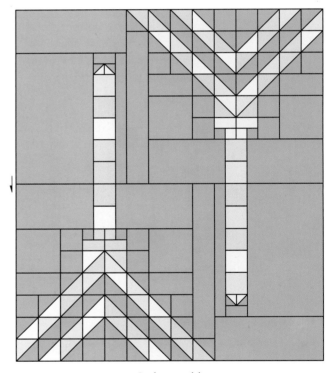

Quilt assembly

10 Refer to "Finishing Your Quilt" on page 78. Quilt as desired and bind using the green 2½"-wide strips.

Blocks and Repeats

Quilts with Block Construction

 FALL LEAVES

DRIP DROP

STONEWORK

THORNY

 SHAKEN OR STIRRED

FALL LEAVES

The brilliant colors, the crisp temperatures, the yummy food—everything about fall is so comforting. I can spend hours drinking coffee and watching brightly colored leaves swirl their way around in the wind. This quilt may look more difficult than it really is. The leaves are simple squares with prairie points sewn into the seams to create the shapes and add dimension. The leaf edges are loose on the quilt top until tacked down when the final quilting is done.

Inspiration: windswept leaves

Materials

Yardage is based on 42"-wide fabric.

4⅛ yards of plum solid for background and binding

25 pairs of matching 5" squares in assorted fall prints*

3¾ yards of fabric for backing

67" x 77" piece of batting

Cardstock or other heavy paper

You can also use 25 squares, 10" x 10".

Cutting

From the plum solid, cut:

5 strips, 2½" x 42"; crosscut into 50 rectangles, 2½" x 4"

3 strips, 4½" x 42"; crosscut into 20 rectangles, 4½" x 5"

4 strips, 4½" x 39"

2 strips, 10½" x 39"

3 strips, 15½" x 42"

7 strips, 2½" x 42"

From *each* pair of 5" squares, cut:

1 square, 5" x 5" (25 total)

2 rectangles, 2½" x 4" (50 total)

"Fall Leaves," designed and pieced by Heather Scrimsher, machine quilted by Pat Derry

Finished quilt: 59" x 69"   **Finished block:** 4½" x 4½"

Making the Prairie Points

After cutting, work at your ironing station to make the prairie points. It's nice to have a slightly hard pressing surface to do this. A spray bottle with water or starch is also helpful.

1 Cut a 2" x 5" piece of cardstock.

2 Place a 2½" x 4" rectangle wrong side facing up on your pressing surface and place the cardstock on top, aligning the long edges along the bottom. Fold ½" of the fabric over the cardstock and press with a dry iron. Remove the cardstock, leaving the fabric folded. Press again, adding a spritz of water, starch, or sizing if desired.

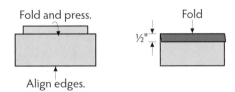

Fold and press.

Align edges.

Fold

½"

3 Fold the fabric in half, wrong sides together and aligning the short raw edges, and press again to mark the center. Open up and fold the corners with the pressed fold down to the center line just created to create a wide triangle.

Center

Fold.   Fold.

4 Fold the triangle in half along the fold line and press again.

Fold.

Raw edges

5 Repeat steps 2–4 to make a total of 50 prairie points from the fall prints and 50 from the plum solid.

Making the Leaf Blocks

Each leaf block has four prairie points, two in matching colors and two in plum solid. The plum prairie points will be pressed toward the print square and the print prairie points will be pressed toward the adjacent plum rectangle or strip. The prairie points are left loose until the quilting is done.

1 Place a plum prairie point on the side of a print 5" square. Align the raw edges and center it; it should be 1½" from each corner. Place a second plum prairie point on the adjacent side of the square, centering it as shown. Pin in place.

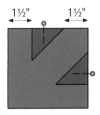

1½"   1½"

2 Add a matching prairie point to each of the remaining two sides of the square. Machine baste the prairie points in place, stitching ⅛" from the edges.

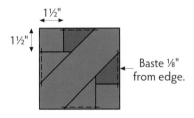

1½"

1½"

Baste ⅛"
from edge.

3 Repeat steps 1 and 2 for all of the 5" squares.

Assembling the Quilt

1 Lay out the leaf blocks in five rows of five blocks each. Place a plum 4½" x 5" rectangle between each block. Rotate each leaf block a quarter turn from the one before it. This adds interest to the quilt.

2 Sew the blocks and plum rectangles together to make a row. Press the seam allowances toward the rectangles. Make five rows.

Make 5.

3 Alternating plum 4½" x 39" strips and the pieced rows from step 2, join the rows and strips. Press the seam allowances toward the plum strips. Press the print prairie points toward the plum fabric and press the plum prairie points toward the leaf blocks.

4 Sew a plum 10½" x 39" strip to each side of the quilt center. Press the seam allowances toward the border strips.

5 Sew the remaining plum 15½"-wide strips together end to end. Trim to make two border strips, each with a length of 59". Sew one to the top of the quilt center, and one to the bottom. Press toward the border strips.

6 Refer to "Finishing Your Quilt" on page 78. Quilt as desired, stitching the prairie points down in the correct direction as you quilt. If you're having a professional quilter complete this step, be sure to provide directions for the prairie points to avoid confusion. Bind using the 2½"-wide strips.

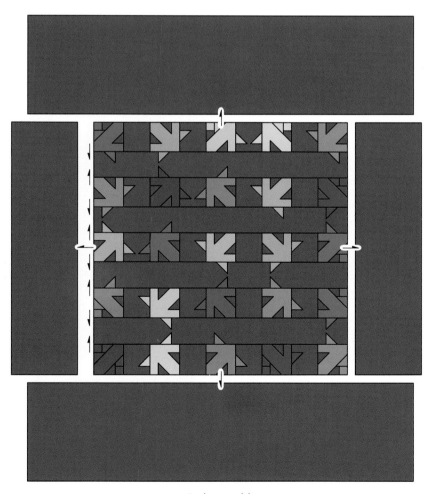

Quilt assembly

DRIP DROP

The magic of rain—it cleanses everything, makes things grow, and creates the perfect day to stay inside and sew! What's not to love, unless you're getting married that day or perhaps your kids have a game and the rain's not quite bad enough to cancel? But we take the good with the bad, and take inspiration from both! Here I looked at a drop of water and put a modern spin on it to design a bright, cheerful homage to rain.

Inspiration: drop of rainwater off a rain chain

Materials

Yardage is based on 42"-wide fabric.

3⅜ yards of cream solid for blocks

⅜ yard *each* of teal, yellow, orange, and magenta print for blocks

½ yard of teal stripe for binding

3¼ yards of fabric for backing

57" x 73" piece of batting

Template plastic

Cutting

Trace the Drunkard's Path patterns on page 39 onto template plastic and cut out.

From the cream solid, cut:
5 strips, 8½" x 42"; crosscut into:
  12 squares, 8½" x 8½"
  12 rectangles, 2½" x 8½"
  24 rectangles, 1½" x 8½"
6 strips, 2" x 42"; crosscut into:
  24 rectangles, 2" x 5"
  24 rectangles, 2" x 3½"
4 strips, 2½" x 42"; crosscut into:
  24 rectangles, 2½" x 3½"
  24 rectangles, 1½" x 2½"
  12 squares, 2½" x 2½"
72 pieces using template A

Continued on page 38

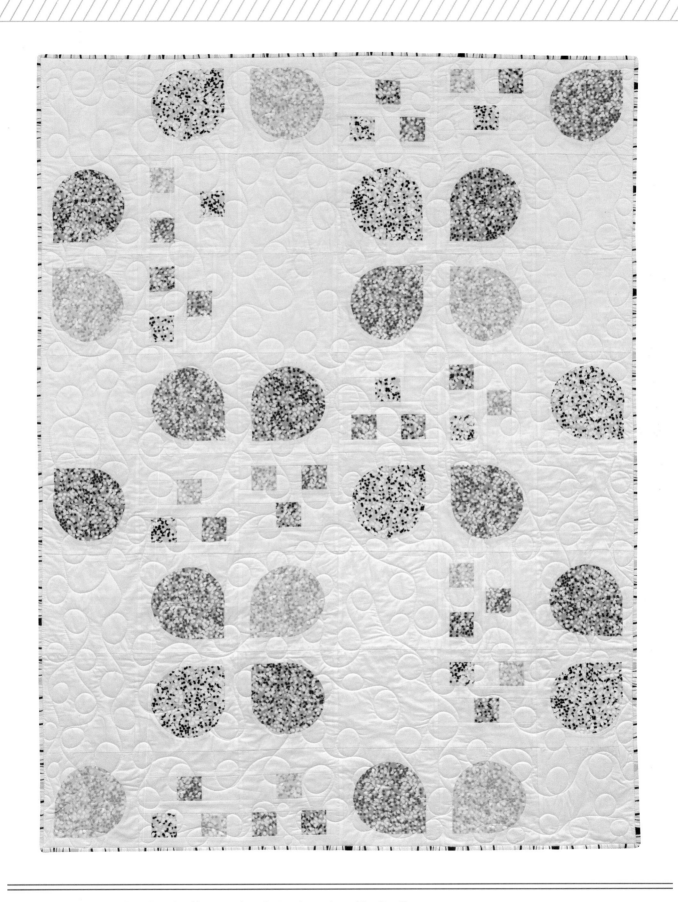

"Drip Drop," designed and quilted by Heather Scrimsher, pieced by Pat Derry

Finished quilt: 48½" x 64½"   **Finished block:** 8" x 8"

Continued from page 36

From *each* of the 4 prints, cut:
    6 squares, 3½" x 3½" (24 total)
    18 pieces using template B (72 total)
    9 squares, 2½" x 2½" (36 total)

From the teal stripe, cut:
    6 strips, 2½" x 42"

Making the Drop Blocks

1 Referring to "Drunkard's Path Units" on page 77, sew the print B pieces to the cream A pieces to make 72 units. Press toward the cream background.

Make 72.

2 Sew a cream 2" x 3½" rectangle to the bottom of each print 3½" square. Press the seam allowances toward the square. Sew a cream-solid 2" x 5" rectangle to the right side as shown and press toward the square. Make six of each different color.

Make 6 of
each color.

3 Arrange three matching Drunkard's Path units together with a unit of the same color from step 2 as shown. Join the units into rows, and then join the rows to create a "drop." Press. Make six of each color.

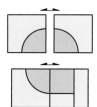

Make 6 of
each color.

4 Trim the blocks to 8½" square, centering the drop. Position the ruler with the 4¼" marks at the center seams. Trim two sides and then rotate the block 180° and trim the remaining two sides.

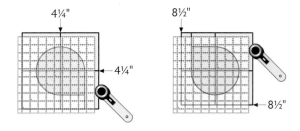

Making the Squares Blocks

1 Sew a cream 2½" x 3½" rectangle to each side of an assorted-print 2½" square. Make three of each color for a total of 12.

Make 12.

2 Randomly select two different-colored print 2½" squares and sew a cream 1½" x 2½" rectangle to each. Sew a unit to each side of a cream 2½" square. Make 12.

Make 12.

3 Arrange a cream 2½" x 8½" rectangle, a unit from step 1, a cream 1½" x 8½" rectangle, a unit from step 2, and a second cream 1½" x 8½" rectangle as shown. Sew the rectangles and units together to make the block. Press the seam allowances in one direction. Make a total of 12 blocks.

Make 12.

Assembling the Quilt

1 Referring to the quilt assembly diagram, arrange the blocks and cream 8½" squares in eight rows of six blocks each, rotating the blocks as shown or as desired. Sew the blocks into rows, and press the seam allowances in opposite directions from row to row. Sew the rows together to complete the quilt top. Press the seam allowances in one direction.

2 Refer to "Finishing Your Quilt" on page 78. Quilt as desired and bind using the striped 2½"-wide strips.

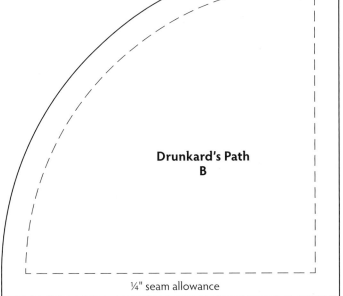

**Drunkard's Path
B**

¼" seam allowance

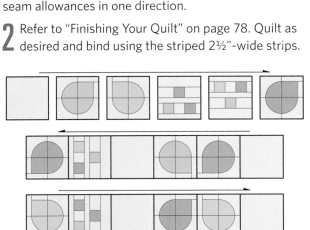

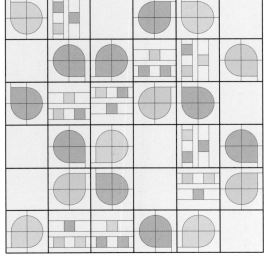

Quilt assembly

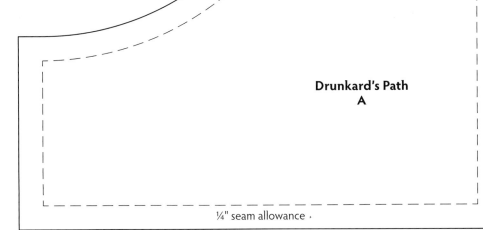

**Drunkard's Path
A**

¼" seam allowance ·

STONEWORK

At one point, when my husband and I were newly married and had bought our first house, I discovered big-box home-improvement stores. More specifically, I found the tile department. Installing squares of tile is like quilting, but once you're done, it's really hard to change your mind. My husband is lucky that I discovered quilting and didn't tile the walls in our bedroom! You'll have fun making this brick-tile inspired quilt . . . just choose some favorite fat quarters, add a solid, and you'll soon have a fabulous quilt.

Inspiration: brick patio pavers

Materials

Yardage is based on 42"-wide fabric. Fat quarters measure 18" x 21".

11 fat quarters of assorted prints for blocks

2 yards of white solid for blocks and sashing

⅝ yard of fabric for binding

4 yards of fabric for backing

72" x 72" piece of batting

Cutting

From *each* of the 11 fat quarters, cut:
    5 strips, 3½" x 21½"; crosscut into:
        9 rectangles, 3½" x 7½" (99 total; 3 are extra)
        6 squares, 3½" x 3½" (66 total; 2 are extra)

From the white solid, cut:
    43 strips, 1½" x 42"; crosscut into:
        9 strips, 1½" x 16½"
        31 strips, 1½" x 15½"
        16 strips, 1½" x 11½"
        64 rectangles, 1½" x 7½"
        48 rectangles, 1½" x 3½"

From the binding fabric, cut:
    7 strips, 2½" x 42"

"Stonework," designed and quilted by Heather Scrimsher, pieced by Robin Rush

Finished quilt: 63½" x 63½"   **Finished block:** 15" x 15"

Making the Blocks

Use a variety of prints for each block. You can choose fabrics in advance or mix them up randomly as you sew. For each block, you will need six assorted 3½" x 7½" rectangles and four 3½" squares. Press all seam allowances toward the assorted prints.

1 Sew two print 3½" squares to opposite sides of a white 1½" x 3½" rectangle. Press.

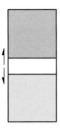

2 Sew a white 1½" x 7½" rectangle and a print 3½" x 7½" rectangle to the right edge of the unit as shown. Press.

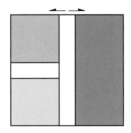

3 Sew a white 1½" x 7½" rectangle and a print 3½" x 7½" rectangle to the bottom of the unit as shown. Press.

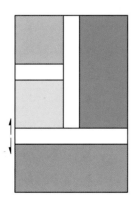

4 Add another white 1½" x 7½" rectangle and a print 3½" x 7½" rectangle to the bottom of the unit. Press.

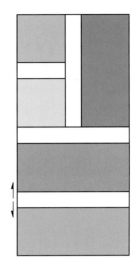

5 Sew a print 3½" square and a print 3½" x 7½" rectangle to opposite sides of a white 1½" x 3½" rectangle as shown. Press. Make two using different prints.

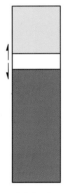

Make 2.

6 Sew the two units from step 5 to opposite sides of a white 1½" x 11½" strip, rotating one of the units 180°. Press.

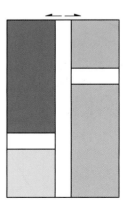

7 Sew a white 1½" x 7½" rectangle and a print 3½" x 7½" rectangle to the top of the unit.

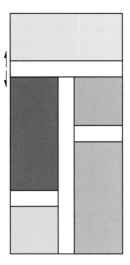

8 Sew the unit from step 4 to the left of a white 1½" x 15½" strip and the unit from step 7 to the right. Press, and the block is done!

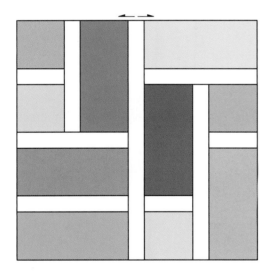

9 Repeat steps 1–8 to make a total of 16 blocks.

Assembling the Quilt

1 Arrange the blocks into four rows of four blocks each and evaluate the placement. Once you're happy with the arrangement, place white 1½" x 15½" strips vertically between the blocks. Place three white 1½" x 16½" strips and one 1½" x 15½" strip horizontally between the blocks as shown in the quilt assembly diagram.

2 Sew the vertical white strips to the right side of three blocks in each row. Press the seam allowances toward the white strips. Do not sew them together yet.

3 Sew the horizontal strips to the top of the blocks in the bottom three rows. Press the seam allowances toward the white strips.

Short Sashing Strips

At a glance, it looks like the rows of blocks in this quilt are separated by full-width white sashing strips. However, to make it easier to align the blocks from row to row so that the final impression is one of accurately laid stonework, I cut sashing strips the same width as the blocks. The effect is a solid white line, but assembling the quilt top is so much easier.

4 Sew the blocks into rows and sew the rows together to complete the quilt top. Press the seam allowances toward the white strips.

5 Refer to "Finishing Your Quilt" on page 78. Quilt as desired and bind using the 2½"-wide strips.

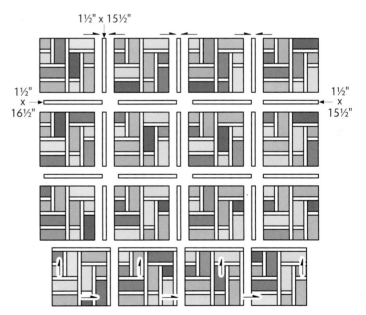

Quilt assembly

THORNY

Shakespeare did a very good job of immortalizing the rose. I too love roses—perhaps remembering the first thrill of getting one from a boyfriend. I also love watching the rosebush bloom in my garden. However, I do not like the thorns. The idea for this quilt was conceived while I contemplated the thorns among the flowers. The blocks require a lot of steps, but the piecing is easy. And, each block is big—you need only four—so the final quilt goes together quickly.

Inspiration: rosebush

Materials

Yardage is based on 42"-wide fabric.

3½ yards of white solid for block background

1⅛ yards of light-yellow solid for blocks

1 square, 10" x 10", *each* of 8 assorted prints for blocks

⅝ yard of fabric for binding

4⅛ yards of fabric for backing

73" x 73" piece of batting

Cutting

From *each* of the 10" squares, cut:
    8 squares, 2⅞" x 2⅞" (64 total)

From the white solid, cut:
    4 strips, 10½" x 42"; crosscut into:
        4 squares, 10½" x 10½"
        16 rectangles, 5½" x 10½"
    3 strips, 5½" x 42"; crosscut into 16 squares, 5½" x 5½"
    5 strips, 2⅞" x 42"; crosscut into 64 squares, 2⅞" x 2⅞"
    16 strips, 2½" x 42"; crosscut into:
        24 rectangles, 2½" x 6½"
        16 rectangles, 2½" x 5½"
        28 rectangles, 2½" x 4½"
        4 rectangles, 2½" x 3½"
        40 squares, 2½" x 2½"
        84 rectangles, 1½" x 2½"

From the light-yellow solid, cut:
    13 strips, 2½" x 42"; crosscut into:
        8 strips, 2½" x 32½"
        8 strips, 2½" x 14½"
        16 rectangles, 2½" x 7½"

From the binding fabric, cut:
    7 strips, 2½" x 42"

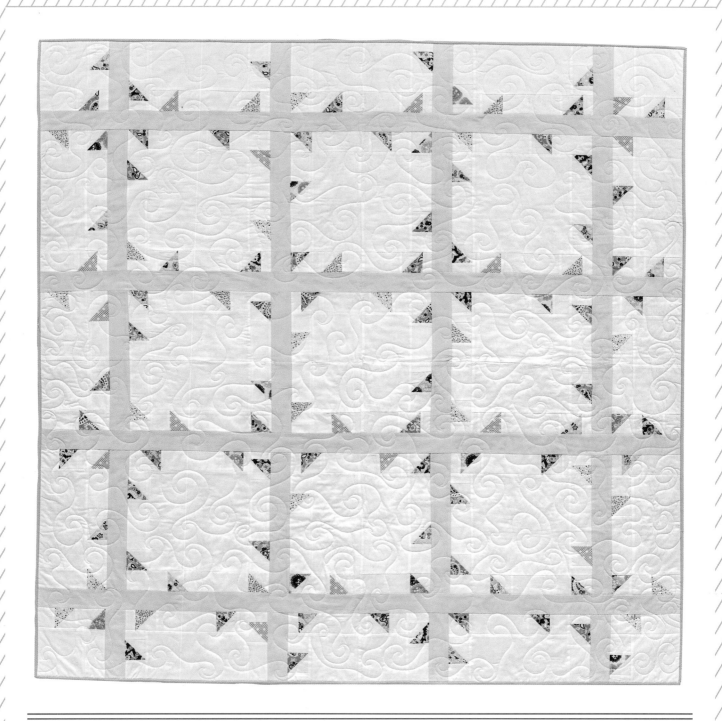

"Thorny," designed, pieced, and quilted by Heather Scrimsher

Finished quilt: 64½" x 64½"   **Finished block:** 32" x 32"

Making Half-Square-Triangle Units

Pair each print 2⅞" square with a white 2⅞" square to make 128 half-square-triangle units. Refer to "Half-Square-Triangle Units" on page 77 for detailed instructions.

Make 128.

Making the Top Block Section

1 Sew a white 1½" x 2½" rectangle to the top of a half-square-triangle unit. Sew a white 2½" square to the bottom as shown. Press the seam allowances toward the white pieces.

2 Sew the unit just made to the right edge of a white 5½" square. Press toward the square.

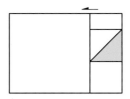

3 Sew a white 2½" x 4½" rectangle to the left of a half-square-triangle unit and a white 1½" x 2½" rectangle to the right side. Join this unit to the unit from step 2. Sew a yellow 2½" x 7½" rectangle to the right edge of the unit. Press according to the arrows. This makes the top-left corner of the block.

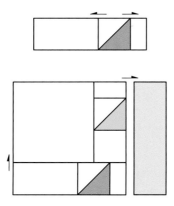

4 For the top center section of the block, join four white 1½" x 2½" rectangles, one white 2½" square, one white 2½" x 4½" rectangle, one white 2½" x 6½" rectangle, and four half-square-triangle units as shown. Sew the units to the right side, bottom, and left side of a white 5½" x 10½" rectangle. Sew a yellow 2½" x 7½" rectangle to the right of the unit.

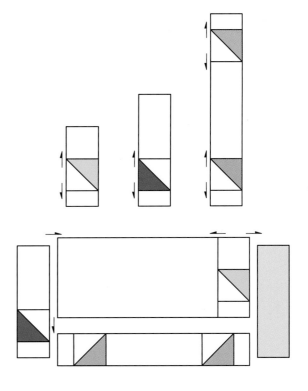

5 Arrange and sew together one white 1½" x 2½" rectangle, two half-square-triangle units, one white 2½" square, one white 2½" x 5½" rectangle, and one white 5½" square as shown to create the top-right corner of the block.

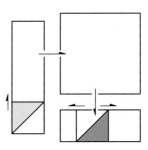

6 Sew the top-left corner section to the left and the top-right corner section to the right of the center section from step 4. Sew a yellow 2½" x 32½" strip to the lower edge to complete the top of the block.

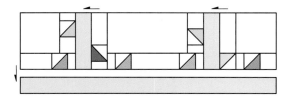

Making the Center Block Section

1 For the left portion of the center section, join four half-square-triangle units, two white 1½" x 2½" rectangles, two white 2½" squares, one white 2½" x 4½" rectangle, and one white 2½" x 6½" rectangle as shown. Sew the units to the top, bottom, and right edge of a white 5½" x 10½" rectangle. Sew a yellow 2½" x 14½" strip to the right of the unit.

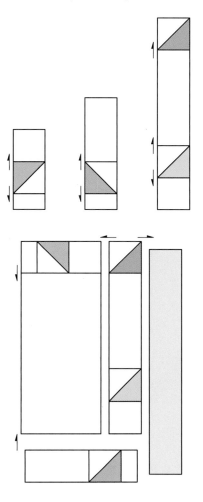

2 For the center section, join five white 1½" x 2½" rectangles, one white 2½" x 4½" rectangle, one white 2½" x 5½" rectangle, three white 2½" x 6½" rectangles, and eight half-square-triangle units as shown. Sew these to a white 10½" square, beginning on the right edge and working clockwise around the square. Add a yellow 2½" x 14½" strip to the right of the unit.

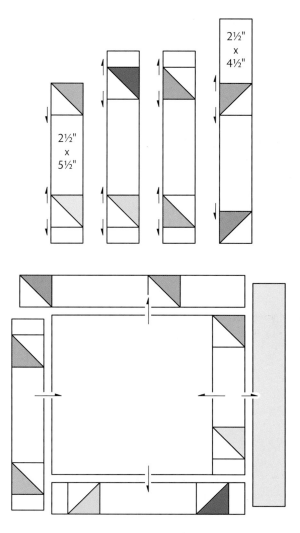

3 To make the right portion of the center section, join four half-square-triangle units, one white 1½" x 2½" rectangle, one white 2½" square, one white 2½" x 3½" rectangle, and two white 2½" x 5½" rectangles as shown. Sew the units to the bottom, left, and top of a white 5½" x 10½" rectangle.

Making the Bottom Block Section

1 To make the bottom-left corner, join two half-square-triangle units, two white 1½" x 2½" rectangles, one white 2½" square, and one white 2½" x 4½" rectangle as shown. Add the units to the top and right of a white 5½" square. Sew a yellow 2½" x 7½" rectangle to the right of the unit.

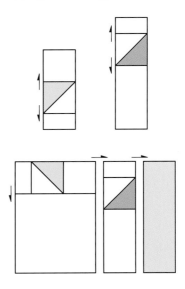

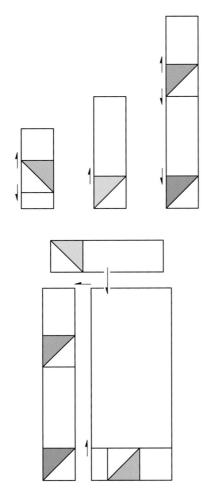

4 Sew the three sections together as shown, and sew a yellow 2½" x 32½" strip to the bottom to make the center section.

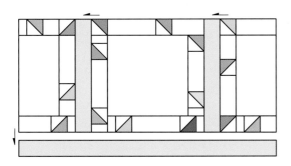

2 To make the bottom center, join four half-square-triangle units, two white 1½" x 2½" rectangles, two white 2½" squares, one white 2½" x 4½" rectangle, and one white 2½" x 6½" rectangle as shown. Add the units to the left, top, and right of a white 5½" x 10½" rectangle. Sew a yellow 2½" x 7½" rectangle to the right of the unit.

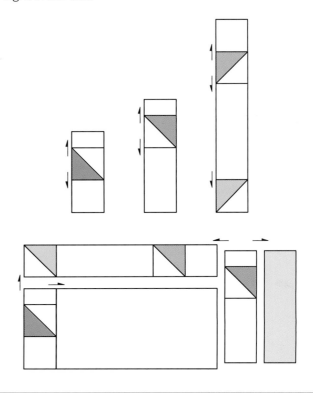

3 To make the bottom-right corner, join two half-square-triangle units, two white 1½" x 2½" rectangles, one white 2½" square, and one white 2½" x 4½" rectangle as shown. Add the units to the left and top of a white 5½" square.

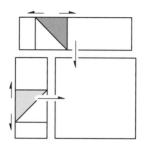

4 Sew the three sections together to make the bottom of the block.

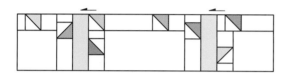

Assembling the Block

1 Sew the top, center, and bottom block sections together.

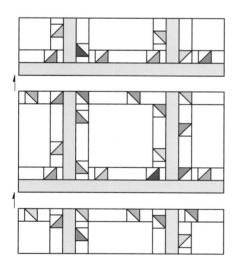

2 Repeat the steps for making the block sections and assembling the block to make a total of four blocks.

Assembling the Quilt

1 Arrange the blocks in two rows of two blocks each. Sew the blocks into rows and sew the rows together to complete the quilt top.

2 Refer to "Finishing Your Quilt" on page 78. Quilt as desired and bind using the 2½"-wide strips.

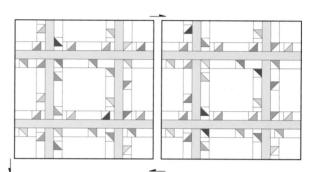
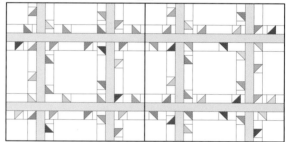

Quilt assembly

SHAKEN OR STIRRED

There is something special about food or drink served in stemware. While I do enjoy martinis, there are times when a fancy, or even an ordinary appetizer or dessert served in a martini glass makes me feel special as well (especially dark-chocolate mousse). This quilt uses a simple block layout, without sashing or borders, so you can easily make it bigger or smaller if you like. And if you're not into martini glasses, think of them as funnels—that works too!

Inspiration: martini glasses

Materials

Yardage is based on 42"-wide fabric.

3¼ yards of white solid for block background

25 assorted print squares, 10" x 10", for glasses

⅝ yard of fabric for binding

4 yards of fabric for backing

68" x 68" piece of batting

Template plastic

Cutting

Trace the pattern on page 54 onto template plastic and cut on the lines to make a template for the glass.

From *each* of the 25 squares, cut:

2 glasses using the template (50 total)

2 rectangles, 1½" x 5½" (50 total)

From the white solid, cut:

5 strips, 5" x 42"; cut into 50 rectangles, 3¾" x 5"

2 strips, 12½" x 42"; cut into 50 strips, 1½" x 12½"

2 strips, 7½" x 42"; cut into 50 rectangles, 1½" x 7½"

7 strips, 5½" x 42"; cut into:

50 rectangles, 1½" x 5½"

50 rectangles, 3½" x 5½"

From the binding fabric, cut:

7 strips, 2½" x 42"

"Shaken or Stirred," designed, pieced, and quilted by Heather Scrimsher

Finished quilt: 60½" x 60½"   **Finished block:** 12" x 12"

Making the Blocks

1 Cut 25 of the white 3¾" x 5" rectangles in half diagonally from corner to corner to make 50 triangles. Cut the remaining 25 in half diagonally in the opposite direction. If you're using a solid that is the same on the right and wrong side, you can cut all the rectangles in the same direction and use the wrong side of the fabric for half of the triangles. If your fabric has distinct right and wrong sides, however, you will need to cut them as shown.

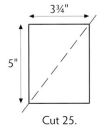
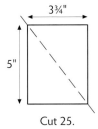

Cut 25. Cut 25.

2 Pin and sew a white triangle to each side of a print glass shape along the diagonal, offsetting the ends of triangles as shown. Press the seam allowances toward the white triangles. The finished unit should measure 4½" x 7½"; trim if needed. Make 50 glass units.

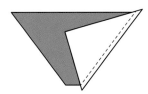

Make 50.

3 Sew a white 1½" x 7½" rectangle to the top of each unit from step 2. Press the seam allowances toward the glass fabric.

4 Sew a white 1½" x 5½" rectangle to the left side of a print 1½" x 5½" rectangle and a white 3½" x 5½" rectangle to the other side as shown. Press toward the print. Make 50 stem units.

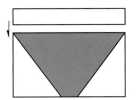

Make 50.

5 To assemble the block, choose two glass units from step 3 and two matching stem units from step 4. Arrange the units as shown and sew together in rows. Sew the rows together, carefully matching the seams of the stem with the bottom of the glass. Press the seam allowances open.

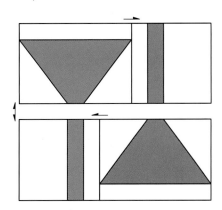

6 Sew white 1½" x 12½" strips to the top and bottom of the block and press the seam allowances toward the strips just added. The block should measure 12½" x 12½". Trim and square up the block if needed.

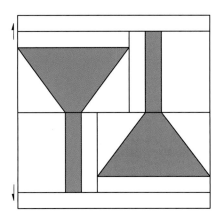

7 Repeat steps 5 and 6 to make a total of 25 blocks.

Assembling the Quilt

1 Arrange the blocks on a design wall in five rows of five blocks each, rotating the blocks as shown in the quilt assembly diagram.

2 Sew the blocks into rows. Press the seam allowances in opposite directions from row to row. Sew the rows together. Press the seam allowances in one direction.

3 Refer to "Finishing Your Quilt" on page 78. Quilt as desired and bind using the 2½"-wide strips.

Quilt assembly

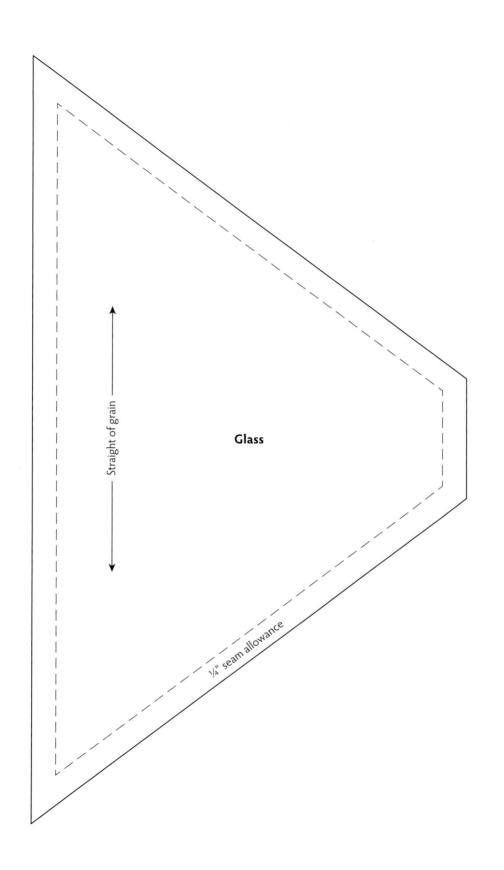

Straight of grain

Glass

¼" seam allowance

Lines and Strips

Quilts with Straight Lines

 FENCE LINE

LAWN

SHUTTERED

MASONRY

 INLAY

FENCE LINE

I don't always love fences, but sometimes the creative design details capture my attention. While I would probably never follow through with it, I always dream of having a very colorful fence. Here I've created it in fabric. This pattern uses freezer paper as a foundation. It helps keep everything under control so your corners match well. The quilt shown would make a striking baby quilt; it's the perfect size to place on the floor for playtime. Simply sew more blocks for a larger version.

Inspiration: neighborhood fence

Materials

Yardage is based on 42"-wide fabric.

1⅓ yards of white solid for block background

1 yard of black solid for sashing, border, and binding

1 strip, 2½" x 42", *each of 2 blue, 2 green, and 4 gray prints for blocks*

3 yards of fabric for backing

53" x 55" piece of batting

Freezer paper, a length of at least 14 feet

Leftover strips from a Jelly Roll would be perfect.

Cutting

From *each* of the gray strips, cut:
   8 rectangles, 2½" x 4" (32 total)

From *each* of the blue strips, cut:
   8 rectangles, 2½" x 5" (16 total)

From *each* of the green strips, cut:
   8 rectangles, 2½" x 5" (16 total)

From the freezer paper, cut:
   16 squares, 10½" x 10½"

From the white solid, cut:
   16 squares, 10" x 10"; cut each in half diagonally to make a total of 32 triangles

From the black solid, cut:
   11 strips, 2½" x 42"; trim 3 of the strips to measure 2½" x 40½"

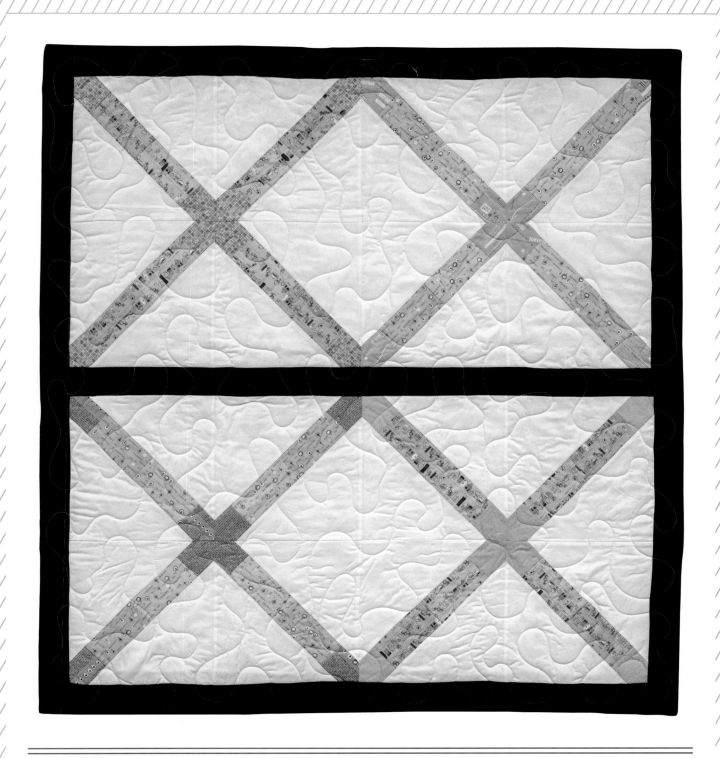

"Fence Line," designed, pieced, and quilted by Heather Scrimsher

Finished quilt: 44½" x 46½"   **Finished block:** 10" x 10"

Making the Blocks

1 Sew two gray 2½" x 4" rectangles, one blue 2½" x 5" rectangle, and one green 2½" x 5" rectangle together as shown. Press the seam allowances in one direction. Make 16 of these pieced strips.

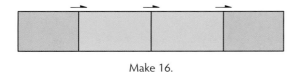

Make 16.

2 On the dull side of each square of freezer paper, use a ruler to mark diagonal lines from corner to corner in each direction. Draw two more lines 1¼" from each side of one diagonal line. Make your lines dark enough so that you can see them from the other side. Turn the freezer paper over so the shiny side is up.

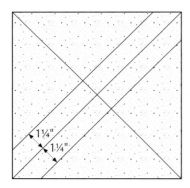

3 Place one of the strips made in step 1 between the 1¼" lines, matching the seam line between the green and blue fabrics with the center line going in the opposite direction. Lightly press the strip to adhere it to the freezer paper.

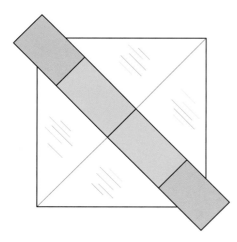

4 Place a white 10" triangle along the strip, right sides together and raw edges aligned. To easily center the triangle, fold it in half to mark the center of the long side. Align the fold with the diagonal line on the freezer paper. Do a test flip to make sure the triangle will cover the freezer paper after it is sewn.

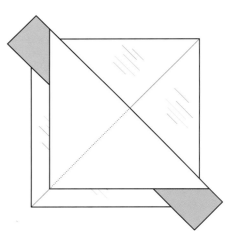

5 Set the stitch length on your machine shorter than you normally sew, and then sew the white triangle to the pieced strip, through the freezer paper. Press the white triangle toward the corner. Repeat to sew a second white triangle on the other side.

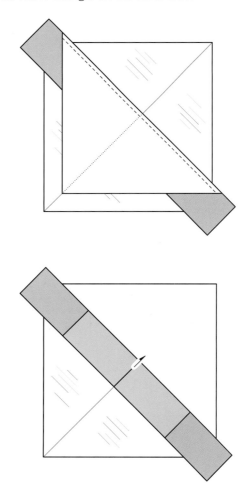

6 Flip the block over and trim the excess around the freezer-paper foundation so that the block measures 10½" x 10½". Crease the freezer paper along each stitching line and carefully remove it. Repeat to make a total of 16 blocks.

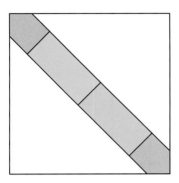

Make 16.

Assembling the Quilt

1 Arrange four blocks together so that they make an X. Pin carefully to match the seams, and then sew the blocks together. I arranged my blocks so that the blues were closer to the center of each group, but you can do the opposite if you prefer. Repeat to make four large X blocks.

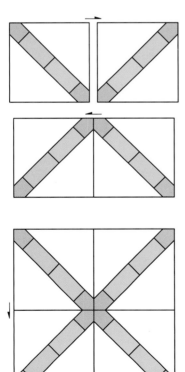

Make 4.

2 Sew the blocks together in pairs.

3 Sew the block pairs to opposite sides of a black 2½" x 40½" strip. Sew black 2½" x 40½" strips to the top and bottom of the block pairs.

4 Join three black 2½" x 42" strips end to end and cut to make two strips, 2½" x 46½". Sew a strip to each side of the quilt.

5 Refer to "Finishing Your Quilt" on page 78. Quilt as desired and bind using the black 2½"-wide strips.

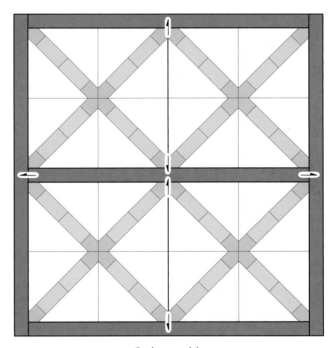

Quilt assembly

LAWN

As the world emerges from winter, Mother Nature paints vivid green landscapes, from tender leaves to newly sprouted grass. The vision of plants waking up is highlighted by the constant colors of the trees that stand steady through all the seasons. This quilt looks lovely made from scraps. If you have a stash, this is a great way to use the greens in your collection.

Inspiration: dark tree trunks against green lawn

Materials

See "Selecting Fabric and Determining Color" at right. Yardage is based on 42"-wide fabric. Fat quarters measure 18" x 21".

15 fat quarters of assorted green prints for patchwork

2 yards of brown solid for tree trunks

⅔ yard of green solid for binding

5½ yards of fabric for backing

69" x 99" piece of batting

Selecting Fabric and Determining Color

When selecting fabrics for this quilt, it's fun to experiment with colors and prints. While you can use all solids for this quilt, prints and tone on tones offer texture and widen your fabric options. I suggest looking at a fabric and immediately naming its color. If it contains multiple colors, it may not be a good candidate for this project. If it's an immediate "green," then it's a good choice. Green can extend from yellow-green to green to blue-green and all will look lovely in this quilt. Little bits of other colors like black or red won't detract from the overall quilt as long as the fabric can be described as "green." Feel free to add more than 15 different fabrics into the mix; more will simply enhance the texture.

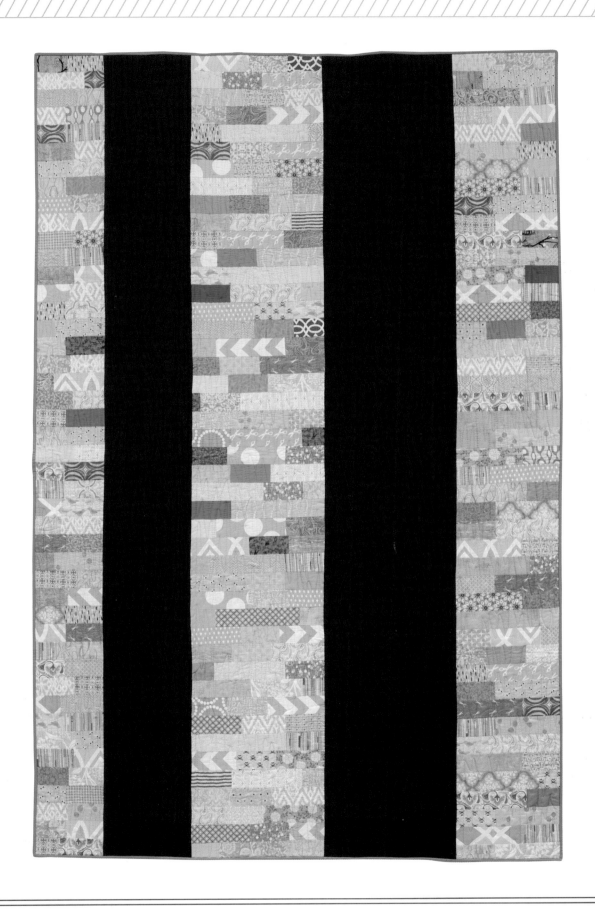

"Lawn," designed, pieced, and quilted by Heather Scrimsher

Finished quilt: 60½" x 90½"

Cutting

See the cutting guide below before cutting the fat quarters.

From *each* of the fat quarters, cut:

    3 strips, 2½" x 8" to 9"* (45 total)

    3 strips, 2½" x 9" to 10"* (45 total)

    15 rectangles, 2½" x 5" (225 total)

From the brown solid, cut:

    2 strips, 15½" x 42"

    2 strips, 10½" x 42"

    1 strip, 12" x 42"; crosscut into:

        1 rectangle, 12" x 15½"

        1 rectangle, 10½" x 12"

From the green solid, cut:

    8 strips, 2½" x 42"

Vary the lengths.

2½" x 10"	2½" x 9"
2½" x 10"	2½" x 9"
2½" x 10"	2½" x 9"
2½" x 5"	

Cutting guide

Making the Columns

1 Randomly select two green 2½" x 5" rectangles and sew them together along the short sides to form a 2½" x 9½" unit. Press the seam allowances to one side. Make 45 units. Trim the units to measure 2½" x 8½". Cut the extra length off one end, or both ends. Vary the cutting so that not all are alike. If you're working with scraps, feel free to sew shorter and longer pieces together. Just be sure to trim each unit to 8½" long.

Make 45.

2 Randomly select a 2½" x 9" to 10" strip and a 2½" x 5" rectangle and sew them together along the short sides. Press the seam allowances to one side. Make 45 units. Trim the units to measure 2½" x 12½", varying the cutting as in step 1.

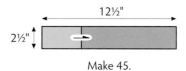

Make 45.

3 Randomly select two 2½" x 5" rectangles and one 2½" x 8" to 9" strip and sew them together along the short sides. This can be in any arrangement you choose; the larger piece can be in the middle or on the end of the smaller strips. Press the seam allowances to one side. Make 45 units. Trim the units to measure 2½" x 15½".

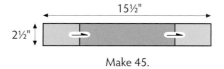

Make 45.

Make It Scrappy!

"Lawn" would be beautiful made as a completely scrappy quilt. I save my scraps from other projects and keep them organized in bins in my sewing room, each bin holding a designated fabric color. Any scrap or strip that can't be folded nicely is tossed into a bin. When one bin gets full, I start evaluating project options. My version of "Lawn" is made entirely from scrap-bin fabrics. I started sewing green scraps together, and then trimming or cutting as needed until I had large sections of "grass." I love spotting some of my favorite fabrics in this quilt—pieces left over from a baby quilt or a favorite bag. If you don't have enough of one color to do a whole scrappy quilt, join forces with a friend! Other quilters are often happy to share scraps or to arrange a trade. Having another quilter's fabric scraps in addition to your own adds a lot of depth and character.

4 Lay out all the 8½"-long units from step 1 to form a column. Sew the units together along their long sides to form a single piece, 8½" x 90½". Press the seam allowances to one side. Repeat with the 12½"-long and 15½"-long units. When finished, you'll have three pieced columns: one 8½" x 90½", one 12½" x 90½", and one 15½" x 90½".

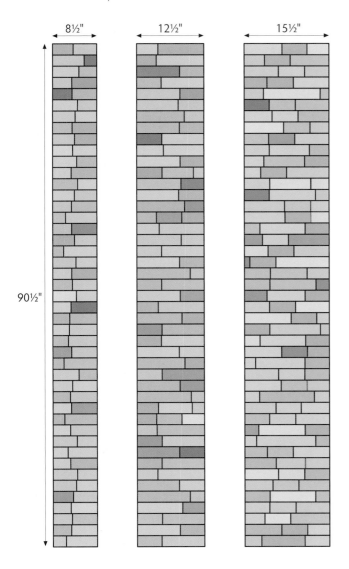

Assembling the Quilt

1 Join the two brown 10½" x 42" strips and the 10½" x 12" rectangle along the short sides. Press the seam allowances to one side. Repeat with the two brown 15½" x 42" strips and the 12" x 15½" rectangle. Trim the strips to 90½" long.

2 Join the brown strips and pieced columns as shown, pressing the seam allowances toward the brown strips.

3 Refer to "Finishing Your Quilt" on page 78. Quilt as desired and bind using the green 2½"-wide strips.

Quilt assembly

SHUTTERED

Every part of the country has its own unique style. Plantation shutters are one of the features you find in many homes in the South. I love them. They seem so classic and pretty with sunlight filtering through. I've taken that classic look and translated it into a quilt made of solid-colored fabrics; it's modern and a bit edgy.

Inspiration: plantation shutters

Materials

Yardage is based on 42"-wide fabric.

3⅛ yards of gray solid for background

⅞ yard of yellow solid for shutters

1¼ yards of black solid for shutters and binding

4 yards of fabric for backing

71" x 75" piece of batting

Cutting

From the yellow solid, cut:
16 strips, 1½" x 42"; crosscut into 64 rectangles, 1½" x 9½"

From the gray solid, cut:
2 strips, 10½" x 42"
4 strips, 5½" x 42"
16 strips, 3½" x 42"; crosscut into 64 rectangles, 3½" x 9½"
1 strip, 2½" x 42"; crosscut into 4 rectangles, 2½" x 9½"

From the black solid, cut:
12 strips, 1½" x 42"
7 strips, 2½" x 42"

"Shuttered," designed and quilted by Heather Scrimsher, pieced by Heather Scrimsher and Chris Warnick

Finished quilt: 62½" x 66½"

Assembling the Quilt

1 Sew a yellow 1½" x 9½" rectangle to the top of a gray 3½" x 9½" rectangle. Make 64 of these units.

Make 64.

2 Sew 16 units together into a column. Sew a gray 2½" x 9½" rectangle to the top as shown. Press the seam allowances toward the gray rectangles. Make four columns.

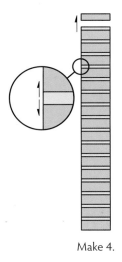

Make 4.

3 Sew the black 1½" x 42" strips together end to end in pairs. Make six and trim each to 1½" x 66½".

4 Sew two columns from step 2 together with three black 1½" x 66½" strips. Make sure that the gray 2½"-high rectangle is on the same end of each column. Press the seam allowances toward the black strips. Make two of these shutter units.

Make 2.

5 Sew the two gray 10½" x 42" strips together along the short ends; cut the pieced strip to 10½" x 66½". Sew two gray 5½" x 42" strips together along the short ends; cut the pieced strip to 5½" x 66½". Make two of the 5½"-wide strips.

6 Arrange the shutter units, the gray 10½" x 66½" strip, and the two gray 5½" x 66½" strips as shown. Rotate one shutter unit so that the gray 2½" pieces are at the opposite end. This will offset the yellow slats a bit. Sew the columns together and press the seam allowances toward the black strips.

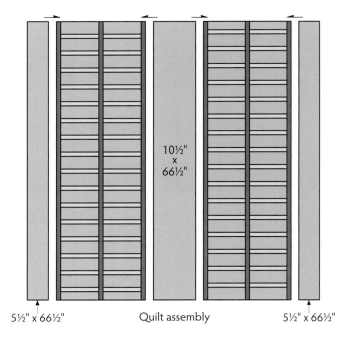

5½" x 66½"   Quilt assembly   5½" x 66½"

7 Refer to "Finishing Your Quilt" on page 78. Quilt as desired and bind using the black 2½"-wide strips.

MASONRY

Older homes and public buildings often have trim features that are part of the actual structure. The result is stunning, yet the element is simple. I saw this building while on vacation in Savannah, Georgia. The quilt from this inspiration makes a fantastic, fast project, and when done in "masculine" fabrics, it also makes a great guy quilt. In fact, this one is destined to be my husband's personal quilt, the one that he claimed as soon as it was done.

Inspiration: corner of historic building

Materials

Yardage is based on 42"-wide fabric.

1 yard* *each* of 5 assorted light prints for blocks

1 yard* *each* of 5 assorted dark prints for blocks

⅔ yard of fabric for binding

4½ yards of fabric for backing

78" x 81" piece of batting

If your fabric measures 44" to 45" wide, ½ yard will be enough.

Cutting

From *each* light and dark print, cut:

  2 strips*, 10½" x 42" (10 light, 10 dark total)

  2 strips*, 4½" x 42" (10 light, 10 dark total)

From the binding fabric, cut:**

  8 strips, 2½" x 42"

If your fabric is at least 42" long after prewashing and removing selvages, 1 strip of each will be enough (5 light and 5 dark total).

**You can also use leftovers from the block prints, as shown in the photo, to make a scrappy binding. You'll need 2½"-wide strips to total 300".*

"Masonry," designed, pieced, and quilted by Heather Scrimsher

Finished quilt: 70½" x 72½"   **Finished block:** 14" x 8"

Assembling the Quilt

1 Pair each light print with a dark print. Sew a dark 10½" x 42" strip to a light 4½" x 42" strip along the long sides. Press the seam allowances toward the dark print. Make two of these strip sets. Sew a matching light 10½" x 42" strip to a matching dark 4½" x 42" strip. Press the seam allowances toward the dark print. Make two of these strip sets. (You will need only one strip set of each if your strips are 42" long.) Cut a total of nine segments, 4½" wide, from each of the two different strip sets.

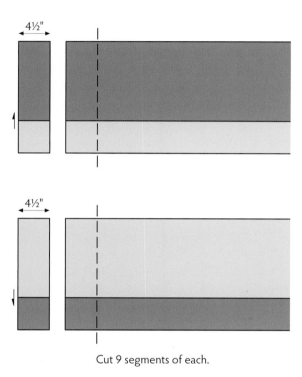

Cut 9 segments of each.

2 Sew two segments together to make a block that measures 8½" x 14½". Press, referring to "Pressing Advice" above right. Make nine blocks.

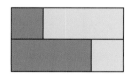

Make 9.

3 Repeat steps 1 and 2 for all of the paired strips to make a total of 45 blocks.

Pressing Advice

Before pressing the seam allowances of your blocks, decide how you will arrange the five columns of blocks. Press the seam allowances toward the darker rectangle in blocks for columns 1, 3, and 5. Press seam allowances toward the lighter rectangle in blocks for columns 2 and 4. This will enable the seam allowances to butt together for easier sewing and less bulk. Another option is to press all of the block seam allowances open.

4 Sew nine matching blocks into a column. Make five columns. Press the seam allowances in opposite directions from column to column. Join the columns and press the seam allowances in one direction.

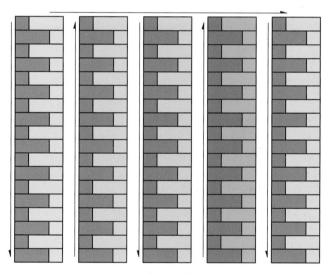

Quilt assembly

5 Refer to "Finishing Your Quilt" on page 78. Quilt as desired and bind using the 2½"-wide strips.

Make It Scrappy

If you have extra fabric, consider making the binding using the leftovers from the block fabrics, as I did.

INLAY

One of my favorite details in the house we recently moved into is a pretty hardwood inlay in the entryway floor. When my quilter friends were visiting and helping me unpack fabric, each one of them asked when I was going to make a quilt based on the floor design. Once the seed was planted, it didn't take me long to create a pattern and make the quilt. This quilt is a bit more advanced due to the angles, and it requires that you become familiar with the 30° and 60° marks on your quilting ruler. That's easily done, though, so don't be intimidated!

Inspiration: wood-floor inlay

Materials

Yardage is based on 42"-wide fabric.

3 yards of white solid for borders

2⅜ yards of yellow solid for block background, borders, and binding

2 squares, 10" x 10", *each* of 6 colors for patchwork

4 yards of fabric for backing

68" x 77" piece of batting

Template plastic

Cutting

Trace the patterns for the triangle, small trapezoid, and large trapezoid (pages 74 and 75) onto template plastic and cut out to make templates.

From *each* 10" square, cut:

2 triangles using the template (24 total)

Continued on page 72

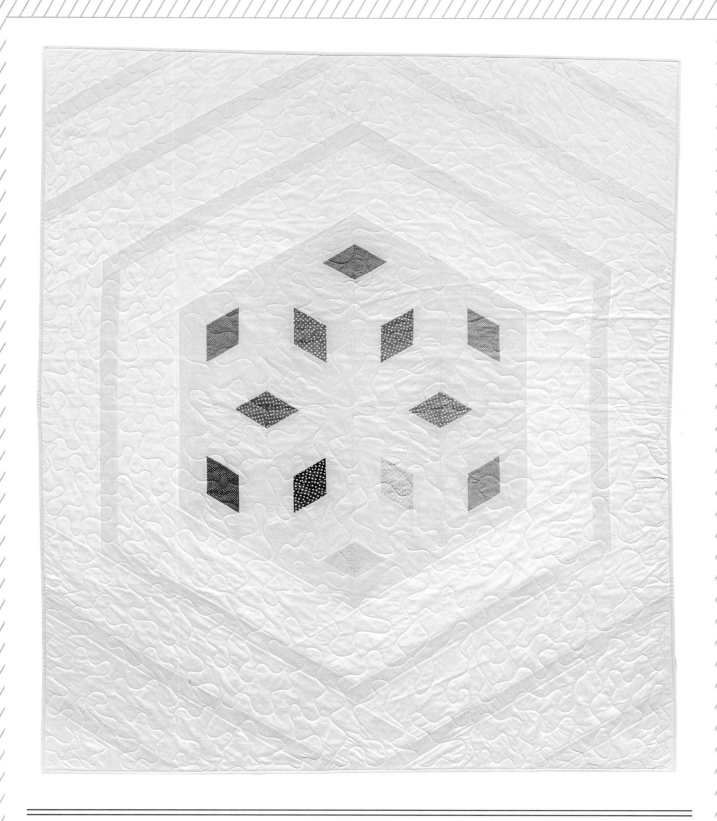

"Inlay," designed, pieced, and quilted by Heather Scrimsher
Finished quilt: 60" x 69"

Continued from page 70

From the yellow solid, cut:

11 strips, 3" x 42"; from the strips cut 24 small and 24 large trapezoids using the templates

12 strips, 2" x 42"

From the white solid, cut:

15 strips, 6½" x 42"; cut *1* of the strips in half

From the binding fabric, cut:

7 strips, 2½" x 42"

Assembling the Hexagon Center

1 Stitch a print triangle to a small yellow trapezoid as shown. Press the seam allowances open.

2 Sew a large yellow trapezoid to the adjacent side of the unit from step 1. Press the seam allowances open. Make a total of 24 triangle units.

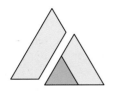

Make 24.

3 Arrange the triangle units in four rows on a design wall as shown above right, matching the triangle centers. You'll have two rows of five triangles and two

rows of seven. Sew the triangles into rows and press the seam allowances open. Sew the rows together to form a hexagon. Press the seam allowances open.

Assembling the Quilt

To assemble the quilt, add border strips to each side and trim them to fit as you go. Use the 30° and 60° lines on your quilting ruler to keep the angles of the cuts accurate. Sew with a slightly shorter stitch length on your machine, and press all seam allowances toward the strip just added.

1 Position the large hexagon so that two flat sides are vertical and there is a "point" on the top and bottom. Center and sew white 6½" x 21" strips to the right and left sides. Press.

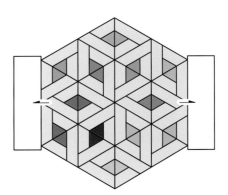

2 Align the 60° line of your ruler with a row seam line from step 1 as shown and trim the white strip along the top. Rotate the quilt and repeat to trim the other border ends.

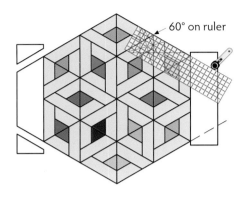

60° on ruler

3 Working clockwise, sew a white 6½" x 42" strip to the adjacent edge, overlapping the first white strip. Press and trim, using the 60° angle mark as before. Save the remainder of the trimmed strips for use in the corners of the quilt. Repeat on the opposite side of the hexagon.

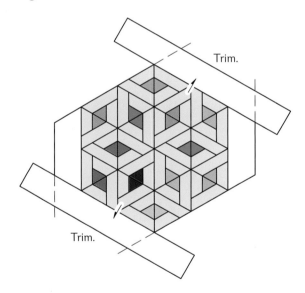

Trim.

Trim.

4 Sew a white 6½" x 42" strip to each of the remaining two sides, and trim as before.

5 Repeat steps 1–4 with the yellow 2" x 42" strips, beginning on the same side and sewing strips in the same order. Refer to the quilt assembly diagram on page 74.

6 Add a second round of white 6½" x 42" strips in the same order and trim.

7 For the next round (beginning with number 19 in the assembly diagram), add one yellow 2" x 42" strip to the top-right side of the hexagon, skipping the vertical sides. Press. Align the 30° angle line of your ruler with the seam just pressed. Adjust the ruler so that there will be a ¼" seam allowance beyond the point of the hexagon. Trim the yellow strip even with the edge of the ruler. Trim the other end of the strip using the 60° angle line of your ruler, aligning it with the seam of the yellow strip.

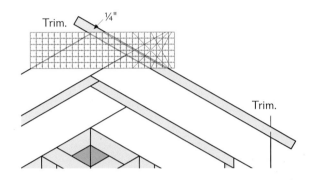

Trim. ¼"

Trim.

Beware of Bias Edges

Take extra care when trimming and handling the quilt as you add the white and yellow borders. Most of the edges of the quilt top will be bias, and will easily stretch out of shape if not handled very carefully. After the quilt top is squared up, it's a good idea to stay stitch a scant ¼" from the edges. This will also help keep your seams from coming apart along the sides during the quilting process.

8 Repeat step 7 to add a yellow strip to the adjacent side of the quilt.

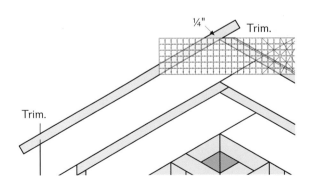

¼" Trim.

Trim.

9 Repeat steps 6 and 7 to add yellow strips to the bottom of the quilt.

10 Add a white 6½" x 42" strip to each corner, press, and trim as before.

11 Add another round of yellow strips, pressing and trimming as before. Finish the corners with the remainder of the white strips. Press, trim, and square up the corners.

12 Refer to "Finishing Your Quilt" on page 78. Quilt as desired and bind using the 2½"-wide strips.

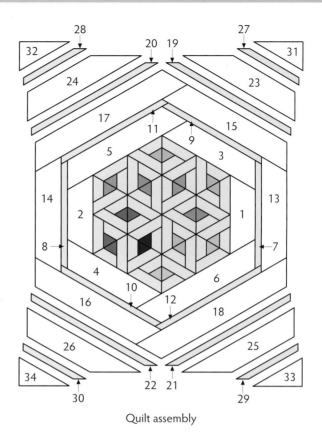

Quilt assembly

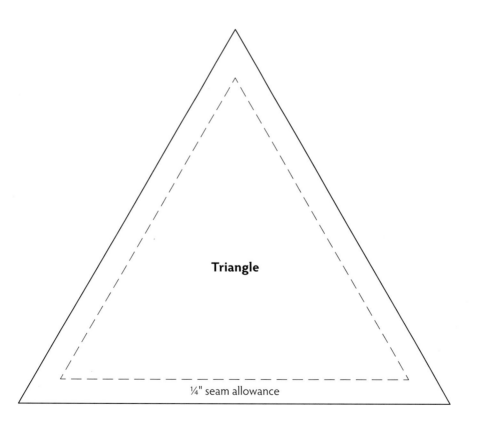

Triangle

¼" seam allowance

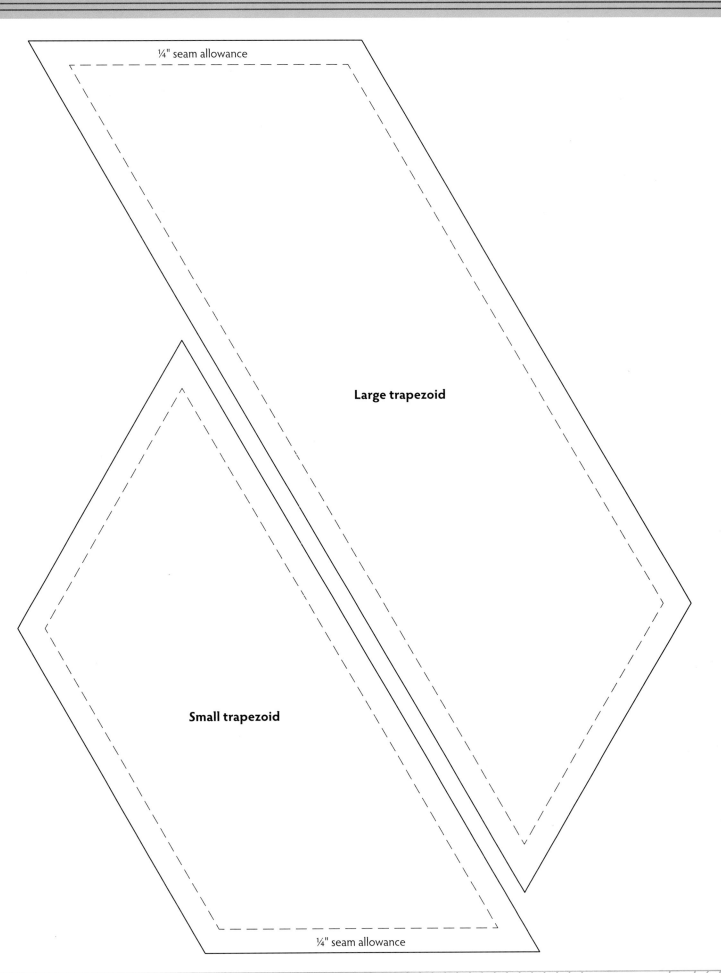

¼" seam allowance

Large trapezoid

Small trapezoid

¼" seam allowance

QUILTMAKING BASICS

In this section I'll share with you some of the knowledge I've gained through experience. If you prefer your own methods, please feel free to ignore any of the instructions you find here. If you can't find the answers you're looking for, please visit ShopMartingale.com for an excellent online quilting resource.

The Very Basic Tools and Supplies

All patterns in this book assume a ¼"-wide seam allowance. If you have problems with maintaining that, nearly every brand of sewing machine has a ¼" presser foot that can make it easier for you. Check with your sewing-machine dealer if you think this might be helpful. Also, it really helps to check your accuracy every so often. I find that I often slip into a "generous" ¼" seam allowance.

A sharp **sewing-machine needle** is very important. Change your needle frequently, not just when one breaks. It really does make your machine happy. The only exception is when sewing on paper foundations—don't bother changing the needle until you're done.

As for **thread,** I like most all of the higher-quality brands. Better-quality thread creates less lint, and the thickness is consistent, helping your seam allowances lie flat. For piecing I usually prefer a fine, 50-weight thread. Experiment to find what you like best, or use your favorite.

Fabric, oh lovely fabric. I have a bit of this in my possession. Not nearly enough, unless you were to ask my husband; he might disagree. I love visiting the local quilt stores and picking out new goodies. And I often visit fabric stores when I'm traveling too. I really enjoy supporting local businesses. It's hard work to run a quilt store, and I appreciate the efforts that shop owners make to provide wonderful fabrics, notions, and other supplies. Each one presents a particular artistic approach to quiltmaking and has a unique inventory.

Many quilts that you see in this book use a specific line of fabric that you may have trouble finding. Fabrics are printed for only a short amount of time, so you may not find the same prints that I used. If in doubt, ask for help at your local quilt shop. Most shop personnel LOVE to help other quilters select fabrics for quilts. If you adore a certain fabric, check for new lines by the same designer. Often the colors and styles of one line of fabric are carried through the next few lines.

Basic supplies that I can't do without include:
- Iron and spray bottle for water and spray starch
- Rotary cutter and mat
- Seam ripper
- Sharp scissors
- Square ruler and longer ruler for cutting

One of my favorite items in my sewing studio is the **design wall.** I made it out of ½"-thick rigid foam insulation (about $10 for a huge sheet at any large home-improvement store) covered with cheap flannel. I find it invaluable to keep track of random pieces and to lay out a quilt to test for color balance before sewing it together. The design wall functions similarly to a child's felt board. Fabric patches and blocks readily stick to the flannel without pins. Larger pieces can be held in place using pins stuck into the foam insulation. If you don't have a permanent sewing area, try a collapsible version, or do what one of my friends does and use a flannel-backed tablecloth taped to the wall with the flannel side out. This works well for her and can be stored easily when not in use.

Pressing

Pressing is very important. Always press after sewing each seam. Don't move your iron across your fabric as you do when ironing clothing; that can distort the pieces. Instead, pick up the iron and move it from place to place, pressing each time you put the iron on the fabric. Rather than using the steam function on my iron, I prefer to use a spray bottle of water to spritz the fabric for perfectly flat results.

A word about spray starch: If you are ever having problems with unruly fabric, fabric that's just not behaving as you want it to, this can bring it under control very quickly. It can also help stabilize your fabrics before cutting to improve accuracy. Spray sizing is another option, especially if you've prewashed your fabric. It adds body to the fabric and makes it easier to cut and piece. Always use a good-quality starch and test it first on a scrap of fabric to make sure it will not damage your fabric. Press carefully so that you don't distort or scorch your fabrics. You'll also need to wash the finished quilt after quilting and binding to remove the starch.

There are many debates about pressing seam allowances open or to one side. Originally batting was loose, so pressing the seam allowances open provided a perfect escape avenue for batting. With today's batting, pressing open or to the side becomes more of a preference. I practice both. I love the crisp finish of pressing the seam allowances open, and it can help minimize bulk when you have several seams meeting. But pressing to the side results in fewer singed fingers and makes matching seams easier.

Pressed to one side   Pressed open

Piecing Essentials

When piecing, I like to chain piece whenever possible. I prepare a stack of fabrics ready to be sewn together and begin stitching. Instead of cutting the thread between each piece, I load the next pair of fabrics at the start of the presser foot, take two or three stitches, and then sew the next pair. When I'm all finished, I remove the chained pieces and clip the long string apart. When doing this, I use a slightly shorter stitch length; this makes it easier to clip the thread between each of the units.

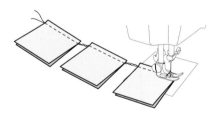

Half-Square-Triangle Units

I admit that triangles and I are not good friends, but I love to include them in my quilts, so we have a truce. While there are a variety of ways to make the half-square-triangle units, the only method I use is to cut and sew squares first. With this method, you'll cut two contrasting squares, sew them together on the diagonal, and cut them apart. The result will be two identical half-square-triangle units.

1 Determine the finished size of the half-square-triangle unit (the size in the quilt top), then add ⅞" to that measurement for the size square to cut. Cut one square each from two different fabrics. As an example, if you need a 2" finished half-square-triangle unit, start with one 2⅞" square of each fabric.

2 Draw a diagonal line from corner to corner on the wrong side of the lighter square. Place the squares right sides together, aligning the raw edges.

3 Stitch ¼" from the drawn line on both sides. Cut on the marked line.

4 Press the seam allowances toward the darker fabric. Measure to make sure the units are the size that you need. All done!

Drunkard's Path Units

Drunkard's Path is one of my favorite blocks of all time. Yes, it involves curved piecing, but once you get the hang of it, the design has so many possibilities. For straight piecing, I don't often use pins, but I do for curved piecing.

One trick to piecing these curves is to mark the center of both pieces. There is always an outside curve and an inside curve. These are also referred to as convex and concave curves.

Convex   Concave

1 Find the center of both curves by folding the pieces in half, finger-pressing a crease, and marking the fold with a pin.

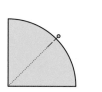

2 Place the two pieces right sides together and match both centers. Pin in the center, and then pin both ends together. Add one or more pins in between, depending on the size of the unit.

3 Sew the pieces together, making sure the pie shape is on the bottom. Use a ¼" seam allowance and a slightly shorter stitch length. Sew slowly and carefully, keeping the raw edges aligned and your seam allowance accurate as you sew.

4 Press the seam allowances to one side, usually away from the pie piece, toward the concave curve. All done—you can breathe now! I'm sure it looks great!

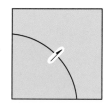

Finishing Your Quilt

After the quilt top is pieced, it's time to create the backing, layer with batting, quilt the layers together, and bind.

Backing

The yardage included in all the projects in this book is for standard, one-seam backing with 4" extra around all sides. Piece your backing with a vertical or horizontal seam, whichever makes best use of your fabric. If you'll be sending your quilt to a professional long-arm machine quilter, be sure to find out how much larger than the quilt top the backing needs to be.

I have made many backings from yardage, and it's certainly the easiest to think about when buying fabric.

However, I've found that I often have large chunks of fabric left over from the current project or even another project. Piecing those together is a perfect way to add interest to the backing. Sometimes I find I love the back as much as the front. Be creative—add in extra blocks from the project or a scrap of your favorite fabric that isn't big enough for another project. There are no set rules on how to piece it together. The diagram below shows some options for piecing yardage.

Two lengths of fabric with a center seam   Partial fabric width

The Quilt Sandwich

This is where the fun begins! I usually complete this step with a visit to a long-arm machine quilter, my checkbook in hand. I love what a professional quilter can do for my quilt. However, I don't always have the time or need for professional quilt finishing, so I follow the steps below to create the quilt sandwich.

1 Lay the backing, wrong side up, on a clean, flat surface. Tape the edges and corners down with masking tape, removing any wrinkles.

2 Check your batting to determine whether there is a right and wrong side. Center the batting, right side up, on top of the backing. Smooth out the batting, and secure with masking tape if needed.

3 Lay the pressed quilt top, right side up, centered on top of the batting. Smooth it out.

4 Baste the layers together with safety pins inserted through all three layers every 4" or so. I use my hand as an approximate guide for this.

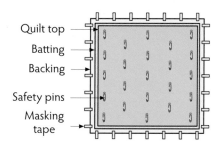

Quilt top
Batting
Backing
Safety pins
Masking tape

Quilting

Most of my quilts are quilted on a long-arm machine, but you can use other methods to keep the layers together. Consider tacking it, or adding buttons. You can use your home sewing machine to quilt simple